BILLY GRAHAM

Unto the Hills

Create in me a clean heart, O God;
and renew a right spirit within me.

PSALM 51:10

How many times in your life have you
wished you could start all over again with
a clean slate, with a new life? Resolve
right now to allow God to wipe your slate
clean by confessing your sins and letting
Him give you a brand new start.

January 1

*For ever, O Lord,
thy word is settled in heaven.*

PSALM 119:89

As the Christian surveys the world scene,
he is aware that we do not worship an
absentee God. He is aware that God is in
the shadows of history and that He has
a plan. No matter how foreboding the
future, the Christian knows the end of
the story of history. We are heading
toward a glorious climax.

December 31

"I am the way, and the truth, and the life; no one comes to the Father, but by me."

JOHN 14:6, RSV

Not only does Christ give directions to the Father through Himself, He also gives us daily directions as to His Father's will for our lives. Determine to follow Christ and never be lost!

January 2

And God shall wipe away all tears from their eyes; and there shall be no more death, neither sorrow, nor crying, neither shall there be any more pain: for the former things are passed away.

REVELATION 21:4

Think of a place where there will be
no sin, no sorrow, no quarrels,
no misunderstandings, no hurt feelings,
no pain, no sickness, no death.
That is heaven!

December 30

For he has said,
"I will never fail you nor forsake you."
Hence we can confidently say,
"The Lord is my helper,
I will not be afraid."

HEBREWS 13:5-6, RSV

Nothing can touch us apart from
God's will. We can be sure that everything
that happens is for the purpose of
building us up. Remember,
God will never fail you or forsake you!

January 3

*He seized the dragon, that ancient
serpent, who is the devil, or Satan,
and bound him for a thousand years...
{where he} will be tormented
day and night for ever and ever.*
REVELATION 20:2,10, NIV

There is One who is more powerful than
Satan! This One defeated him 2,000 years
ago on the cross. Satan suffered his
greatest defeat at the cross, and in the
resurrection of the Lord Jesus Christ.

December 29

What is man,
that thou art mindful of him?

PSALM 8:4

God gave all that He had—
His Son, the Lord Jesus Christ—
because He valued us so highly.
Since God thought this much of us,
shouldn't we show that we value Him by
putting Him first in all that we do—our
family life, our business life,
our spiritual life?

January 4

And there shall be no more curse: but the throne of God and of the Lamb shall be in it; and his servants shall serve him.

REVELATION 22:3

As we approach the end of the age, the head of Satan is being battered and bruised as the forces of God gain momentum. Under the command of God, Michael, the archangel, is organizing his forces for the last battle—Armageddon. The last picture in the Bible is of heaven.

December 28

It is of the Lord's mercies that we are not consumed, because his compassions fail not. They are new every morning: great is thy faithfulness.

LAMENTATIONS 3:22-23

Because God is a person, He feels that which we feel. After all, we are made in His image, so it is to be expected that we would be able to communicate our deepest feelings and emotions to God.

January 5

I pray that out of his glorious riches he may strengthen you with power through his Spirit in your inner being, so that Christ may dwell in your hearts through faith.

EPHESIANS 3:16-17, NIV

We Christians need to rely constantly on the Holy Spirit. It is important that we stand aside and let Him take over in all our choices and decisions.

December 27

Choose this day whom you will serve...
but as for me and my house,
we will serve the Lord.

JOSHUA 24:15, RSV

God commands man to make choices,
but only after providing him with
sufficient information so that his choices
will be informed ones. The choices we
make have the potential for affecting our
lives for better or for worse.

January 6

Be thou faithful unto death,
and I will give thee a crown of life.

REVELATION 2:10

Though you live to be seventy, eighty,
or ninety years old, that is but a snap
of the finger compared to eternity. We
have only a few brief years at the most.
Let's live them for the Lord.

December 26

*Pray without ceasing. In every thing give
thanks: for this is the will of
God in Christ Jesus concerning you.*

1 THESSALONIANS 5:17-18

Praying unlocks the doors of heaven
and releases the power of God.
God's answers are always right and good
and best. Whether prayer changes our
situation or not, one thing is certain:
Prayer *will* change us!

January 7

Wherefore God also hath highly exalted him, and given him a name which is above every name: that at the name of Jesus every knee should bow.

PHILIPPIANS 2:9-10

On that first Christmas night in Bethlehem, "God was manifest in the flesh" (I Timothy 3:16). This manifestation was in the person of Jesus Christ. If you want to know what God is like, then take a long look at Jesus Christ.

December 25

Thou wilt keep him in perfect peace,
whose mind is stayed on thee.

ISAIAH 26:3

Are storms in your life making you afraid?
You can have peace despite the storms.
Stay close to Jesus Christ.
Read God's Word. Pray.

January 8

Ye believe in God, believe also in me.

JOHN 14:1

This sequence of faith is inevitable.
If we believe in what God made
and what God said, we will believe in the
One whom God sent.

December 24

The angel of the Lord encamps around those who fear him, and delivers them.

PSALM 34:7, RSV

Angels are beings who help other people against evil forces and they perform certain duties, without which we could not always be able to achieve a certain goal or station in life. They are just one more example of how God cares for and keeps us against the forces of Satan which are constantly trying to defeat us.

January 9

And the angel said unto them, Fear not:
for, behold, I bring you good tidings of
great joy, which shall be to all people.

LUKE 2:10

The good tidings were that the Savior
had come. The angel message was that
God had come, redemption was
possible, the Lord had visited His
people with salvation.

December 23

*What therefore God hath joined together,
let not man put asunder.*

MATTHEW 19:6

There is no marriage that is beyond repair
in the sight of God. We should first
submit ourselves and then our marriage
to Christ. We must humble ourselves and
lay our pride and our desire to please
ourselves first on His altar. Then God can
restore feelings and bring healing to a
marriage in trouble.

January 10

"She will give birth to a son, and you are to give him the name Jesus, because he will save his people from their sins."

MATTHEW 1:21, NIV

An angel announced His conception and gave Him His name. The heavenly host sang a glorious anthem at His birth. By the extraordinary star, the very heavens indicated His coming. In Himself He was the most illustrious child ever born—the holy child of Mary, the divine Son of God.

December 22

Children are a gift from God;
they are his reward.
PSALM 127:3, TLB

Every material goal, even if it is met,
will pass away. But the
heritage of children is timeless.
Our children are our
messages to the future.

January 11

*For the Lamb which is in the midst
of the throne shall feed them, and
shall lead them unto living fountains
of waters: and God shall wipe away all
tears from their eyes.*

REVELATION 7:17

With this great certainty and assurance,
the future holds no terrors we cannot
face. Thus the Christian should never be
filled with fear, discouragement,
or despondency.

December 21

*Don't worry about anything;
instead, pray about everything;
tell God your needs and don't forget to
thank him for his answers.*

PHILIPPIANS 4:6, TLB

If worry doesn't solve the problem, why worry? Turn to God *first* with your problems, for only He is capable of handling them in a way that will be in your best interest.

January 12

Beloved, I wish above all things that thou mayest prosper and be in health, even as thy soul prospereth.

3 JOHN 2

The Bible teaches that a person is more than just a body—each of us is actually a living soul! The soul demands fellowship and communion with God. It demands worship, quietness, and meditation. Nothing but God ever completely satisfies, because the soul was made for God.

December 20

And when he had spent everything...he began to be in want.

LUKE 15:14, RSV

God has erected signposts along life's road—to help keep us out of trouble. They include reading His Word daily, praying "without ceasing," and determining to seek His will for our lives. Such a path is sure to see us home safely.

January 13

Now it is God who makes both us and you stand firm in Christ. He anointed us, set his seal of ownership on us, and put his Spirit in our hearts as a deposit, guaranteeing what is to come.

2 CORINTHIANS 1:21-22, NIV

God gives us the Spirit not only as a seal, but as a pledge. He is God's down payment, sealing our salvation. He is also God's promise to do everything He says in His Word.

December 19

For the joy of the Lord is your strength.
NEHEMIAH 8:10

Joy cannot be pursued. It comes from
within. It is a state of being.
It does not depend on circumstances,
but triumphs over circumstances.
It produces a gentleness of spirit and
a magnetic personality.

January 14

Lest Satan should get an advantage of us:
for we are not ignorant of his devices.

2 CORINTHIANS 2:11

Satan is indeed capable of doing
supernatural things—but he acts only
by the permissive will of God. It is
God who is all powerful. It is God
who is omnipotent. We are not to be
fearful, distressed, deceived, or
intimidated. Rather, we are to be on
our guard, calm and alert.

House Clean Elnora!

December 18

Know ye not that ye are the temple of God, and that the Spirit of God dwelleth in you?

1 CORINTHIANS 3:16

We know that the body is God's temple. We ought not to cause it to become dirty by doing things to it which can cause harm. Let us correctly pre-judge those persons and places God's Word warns us to avoid, so that we do not get into trouble.

January 15

This is how God showed his love among us: He sent his one and only Son into the world that we might live through him.

1 JOHN 4:9, NIV

The dramatic story of man's lowest depths and God's highest heights can be couched in twenty-five beautiful words: "For God so loved the world, that he gave his only begotten Son, that whosoever believeth in him should not perish, but have everlasting life" (John 3:16).

December 17

Put on the whole armor of God,
that ye may be able to stand against
the wiles of the devil.

EPHESIANS 6:11

Is your home built on a solid foundation?
Today, Satan is attacking the family
as never before. As always,
our best defense is the Word of God.
Read the Bible together as a family.
Have family devotions.
Pray for one another daily by name.

January 16

Hereby we know that he abideth in us,
by the Spirit which he hath given us.

1 JOHN 3:24

The Holy Spirit is already in every
Christian heart, and He intends to
produce His fruit. Only the Holy Spirit
can make possible the
out-living of the in-living Christ.

December 16

Man that is born of a woman is of few days.... Seeing his days are determined, the number of his months are with thee, thou hast appointed his bounds that he cannot pass.

JOB 14:1,5

We should strive to live every day as if it was our last, for one day it will be! I am convinced that when a man is prepared to die, he is also prepared to live.

January 17

Who shall separate us from the love of Christ? ...we are more than conquerors through him who loved us.

ROMANS 8:35, 37

Perhaps you...find yourself almost crushed by the circumstances which you are now facing. Don't despair! God's grace is sufficient for you and will enable you to rise above your trials.

December 15

God is our refuge and strength,
a very present help in trouble.

PSALM 46:1

Like the torch held by the Statue of
Liberty in the harbor, God's light shines
to signify that He is a refuge for all who
wish to flee from the storms of life, "a help
in the time of storms." Cry out to Jesus
and He will answer you.

January 18

Beloved, now are we the sons of God, and it doth not yet appear what we shall be: but we know that, when he shall appear, we shall be like him; for we shall see him as he is.

1 JOHN 3:2

In God's kingdom, Christ is King. When He is sovereign in men's hearts, anguish turns to peace, hatred is transformed into love, and misunderstanding into understanding.

December 14

The wicked is driven away in his wickedness: but the righteous hath hope in his death.

PROVERBS 14:32

For the person who has trusted Christ as Savior, death is only the beginning, not the end. What a glorious thought with which we can comfort ourselves, no matter what our circumstances. We *will* see Christ someday if we have put our faith in Him.

January 19

Love not the world,
neither the things that are in the world.
1 JOHN 2:15

Worldliness is a spirit, an atmosphere, an influence, permeating the whole of life in human society, and it needs to be guarded against constantly. We must make an out-and-out stand for Christ. Our lives must make it plain whose we are and whom we serve!

December 13

So ought men to love their wives
as their own bodies.
He that loveth his wife loveth himself.

EPHESIANS 5:28

Determine to put Christ at the center of
your individual lives and then at the
center of your marriage, and it cannot
fail. Be faithful in your Bible reading and
prayer time as a family and you will build
a fortress around your marriage that can
withstand any storm.

January 20

If we confess our sins,
he is faithful and just,
and will forgive our sins and
cleanse us from all unrighteousness.

1 JOHN 1:9, RSV

If we confess not only our sins
but our mistakes to God, He can make
out of them something for our good
and for His glory.

December 12

Who shall ascend the hill of the Lord? And
who shall stand in his holy place?
He who has clean hands
and a pure heart.

PSALM 24:3-4, RSV

The secret of purity is God.
Get a pure heart from God and you can
be supremely happy no matter what the
circumstances and no matter what is
going on around you.

January 21

*If we walk in the light, as he is in the
light, we have fellowship one with
another, and the blood of Jesus Christ
his Son cleanseth us from all sin.*

1 JOHN 1:7

Where man has failed, God has
succeeded. The Bible says that the blood
of Christ has power to cleanse the
conscience from dead works to serve the
living God. This is not mere theory;
it is a fact of Christian experience.

December 11

And we know that all things work together for good to them that love God, to them who are the called according to his purpose.

ROMANS 8:28

Our hope is not based on circumstance. It is through our adversities that we learn to trust in Jesus. Look upon adversities as an opportunity from God to grow in your faith and to become a stronger servant of His.

January 22

But rejoice that you participate in the sufferings of Christ.

1 PETER 4:13, NIV

Perhaps you are undergoing suffering that you cannot express, even to your dearest friend—an inward, heartrending, heartbreaking suffering. In the midst of it all, there is the promise of victory. Christ has overcome the world, and you, by faith, can overcome the world through our Lord Jesus Christ.

December 10

The Lord is my light and my salvation;
whom shall I fear?

PSALM 27:1

God is able, indeed He is anxious,
to deliver us from all sorts of trouble.
He wants to give us strength to
overcome the temptation to sin which
separates Him from those He loves.

January 23

For he is our peace....
EPHESIANS 2:14

Peace is not man's to give.
It comes from Christ.
Only Christ can cancel sin and create a
peace treaty with God and men.
Do *you* know this peace?

December 9

For I reckon that the sufferings of this present time are not worthy to be compared with the glory which shall be revealed in us.

ROMANS 8:18

Look toward heaven, look beyond the clouds, and you will see that the sufferings that you are undergoing here are nothing compared to the glory that God has prepared for you yonder.

January 24

*Who is gone into heaven, and is
on the right hand of God.*

1 PETER 3:22

The founders of the various non-Christian
religions of the world have lived, died, and
been buried; in some instances, it is still
possible to visit their graves. But Christ is
alive! His resurrection is a fact! His tomb
is empty—and this is a compelling and
central proof of His unique divine nature
as God in human flesh.

December 8

For His anger is but for a moment.
His favor is for a lifetime.

PSALM 30:5, NASB

As we wait upon the Lord, God may
sometimes seem slow in coming to help
us, but He never comes too late.
His timing is always perfect.
How could it not be so from a God who
favors us, as we do our children,
for a lifetime?

January 25

*If ye suffer for righteousness' sake,
happy are ye.... For it is better, if the will
of God be so, that ye suffer for well-doing,
than for evil-doing.*

1 PETER 3:14, 17

A happy life is not one filled only with
sunshine, but one which uses both light
and shadow to produce beauty.
Persecution can become a blessing
because it forms a dark backdrop for the
radiance of the Christian life.

December 7

Into your hands I commit my spirit;
redeem me, O Lord, the God of truth.

PSALM 31:5, NIV

Death for the righteous is distinctively
different from what it is for the
unbeliever. It is not something to be
feared, nor is it to be shunned.
It is the shadowed threshold to the
palace of God.

January 26

But ye are a chosen generation, a royal priesthood, an holy nation, a peculiar people; that ye should shew forth the praises of him who hath called you out of darkness into his marvellous light.

1 PETER 2:9

We, as Christ's followers, will frequently be treated as "peculiar people" and as strangers. We are not to let persecution distract us from our purpose—"to show forth" His praises!

December 6

Blessed is he whose transgression is forgiven, whose sin is covered.

PSALM 32:1

Charles Haddon Spurgeon says,
"Forgiven sin is better
than accumulated wealth.
The remission of sin is infinitely
to be preferred before
all the glitter and the glare
of this world's prosperity.

January 27

*Desire the sincere milk of the word,
that ye may grow thereby.*

1 PETER 2:2

Scripture memorized can come to mind
when you do not have your Bible with
you—on sleepless nights, when driving
a car, traveling, when having to make
an instantaneous important decision.
It comforts, guides, corrects,
encourages—all we need is there.
Memorize as much as you can.

December 5

God commendeth his love toward us,
in that, while we were yet sinners,
Christ died for us.

ROMANS 5:8

God loves, but He also hates. The reason
God hates sin is that it is sin which, left
unforgiven, sends men and women out
into a timeless eternity in hell. God is not
willing that any should perish, but that
all might come to a knowledge of Him.

January 28

He was chosen before the creation of the world, but was revealed in these last times for your sake. Through him you believe in God, who raised him from the dead and glorified him, and so your faith and hope are in God.

1 PETER 1:20-21, NIV

All things were created by Him and He sustains all creation.

December 4

Faith is the substance of things hoped for.
HEBREWS 11:1

God values faith, our trust in Him, above
every other character quality that a
Christian can develop. And how do we
develop faith? By spending time in the
presence of God through prayer and by
applying His Word and His promises to
our everyday lives.

January 29

You were redeemed from the empty way of life handed down to you from your forefathers...with the precious blood of Christ, a lamb without blemish or defect.

1 PETER 1:18-19, NIV

The blood of Christ may seem to be a grim and repulsive subject to those who do not realize its true significance, but to those who have accepted His redemption and have been set free from the slavery of sin, the blood of Christ is precious.

December 3

Looking unto Jesus the author and finisher of our faith....

HEBREWS 12:2

God wants us to look to Jesus, the author and finisher of our faith. He has already overcome similar trials and tribulations and will give us the power to do the same. He waits only to be asked.

January 30

Be ye also patient; stablish your hearts:
for the coming of the Lord draweth nigh.

JAMES 5:8

Jesus Christ is going to come back in person. The Lord Jesus is coming back Himself! That's how much He loves us. The plan of salvation is not only to satisfy us in this world and give us a new life here, but He has a great plan for the future—for eternity!

December 2

Now thanks be unto God, which always causeth us to triumph in Christ.

2 CORINTHIANS 2:14

Christ has triumphed over tragedy and He wants us to do the same because in such triumph God is glorified.
We have the power to triumph over tragedy, even in situations which might seem hopeless and unredeemable.

January 31

Night is coming, when no one can work.

JOHN 9:4, NIV

I wonder how many of us will look back
over a lifetime of wasted opportunities
and ineffective witness and weep because
we did not allow God to use us as He
wanted. If ever we are to study the
Scriptures, if ever we are to spend
time in prayer, if ever we are to win
souls for Christ...it must be *now*.

December 1

For I can do everything God asks me to with the help of Christ who gives me the strength and power.

PHILIPPIANS 4:13, TLB

Christ desires to be with you in whatever crisis you may find yourself. Call upon His name. See if He will not do as He promised He would. He will not make your problems go away, but He will give you the power to deal with and overcome them.

February 1

*Come near to God
and he will come near to you.*
JAMES 4:8, NIV

Incredible as it may seem,
God wants our companionship.
He wants to have us close to Him.
He wants to be a father to us,
to shield us, to protect us, to counsel us,
and to guide us in our way through life.

November 30

*The angel of the Lord encampeth round
about them that fear him,
and delivereth them.*

PSALM 34:7

I have heard or read literally thousands of
stories of people being delivered. Could it
be that these were all hallucinations or
accidents or fate or luck? Or were real
angels sent from God to perform certain
tasks? I prefer to believe the latter.

February 2

*As the body without the spirit is dead,
so faith without works is dead also.*

JAMES 2:26

Salvation is indeed a gift of God,
but there is a sense in which we work
out our own salvation with fear and
trembling. His creative action takes
place through our obedient action,
and He is able to work when we work.

November 29

The Lord is nigh unto them that are
of a broken heart; and saveth such as be
of a contrite spirit.

PSALM 34:18

Before I can become wise, I must first
realize that I am foolish. Before I can
receive power, I must first confess that I
am powerless. I must lament my sins
before I can rejoice in a Savior.
Mourning, in God's sequence, always
comes before exultation.

February 3

What does it profit, my brethren, if a man says he has faith but has not works?

JAMES 2:14, RSV

Good works are not a means of salvation because we are saved by grace through faith. But, our good works are an evidence of salvation; and if we do all the good we can, to all the people we can, at any time we can, by any means we can, we will hear "well done" at the judgment bar of God.

November 28

My soul shall be joyful in the Lord:
it shall rejoice in his salvation.

PSALM 35:9

When Jesus Christ is the source of joy,
there are no words that can describe it.
If the heart has been attuned to God
through faith in Christ, then its overflow
will be joyous optimism and good cheer.

February 4

I have come that they might have life, and that they might have it more abundantly.

JOHN 10:10

There are higher levels of living to which we have never attained. There is peace, satisfaction, and joy that we have never experienced. God is trying to break through to us. The heavens are calling. God is speaking! Let man hear.

November 27

Thy mercy, O Lord, is in the heavens; and thy faithfulness reacheth unto the clouds.

PSALM 36:5

Charles Kingsley sensed this truth when he wrote: "No cloud across the sun but passes at the last and gives us back the face of God once more."

February 5

The testing of your faith produces patience. But let patience have its perfect work, that you may be perfect and complete, lacking nothing.

JAMES 1:3-4, NKJV

Patience is an attitude of expectation. God can produce valuable qualities in our lives through the hurts and suffering we experience. We can suffer patiently, for our suffering will yield a spiritual harvest.

November 26

For with thee is the fountain of life:
in thy light shall we see light.

PSALM 36:9

The happiness which brings enduring
worth to life is not the superficial
happiness that is dependent on
circumstances. It is the happiness and
contentment that fills the soul even in the
midst of the most distressing of
circumstances and the most
adverse environment.

February 6

Blessed is the man who endures trial, for when he has stood the test he will receive the crown of life which God has promised to those who love him.

JAMES 1:12, RSV

To the Christian, death is said in the Bible to be a *coronation*. The Bible says we are pilgrims and strangers in a foreign land. This world is not our home; our citizenship is in heaven. To him who is faithful, Christ will give a crown of life.

November 25

Commit thy way unto the Lord; trust also in him; and he shall bring it to pass.

PSALM 37:5

Two conflicting forces cannot exist in one human heart. When doubt reigns, faith cannot abide. Where hatred rules, love is crowded out. Where selfishness rules, there love cannot dwell. When worry is present, trust cannot crowd its way in.

February 7

My brethren, count it all joy when ye fall into divers temptations.

JAMES 1:2

Few men suffered as the apostle Paul did, yet he learned how to abound and how to be abased. He learned to live above his circumstances—even in a prison cell. You can do the same. Refuse to permit circumstances to get you down. In the midst of your difficulties, there will be a deep joy.

November 24

Mark the perfect man, and behold the upright: for the end of that man is peace.

PSALM 37:37

"Some day," D. L. Moody said, "you will read in the papers that D. L. Moody of East Northfield is dead. Don't you believe a word of it. At that moment I shall be more alive than I am now. I shall have gone up higher, that is all—out of this old clay tenement into a house that is immortal."

February 8

There is laid up for me a crown of righteousness, which the Lord, the righteous judge, shall give me at that day: and not to me only, but unto all them also that love his appearing.

2 TIMOTHY 4:8

George Whitefield, the great English evangelist, said, "I am daily waiting for the coming of the Son of God." He burned out his life in proclaiming the gospel of Christ. Can we do less?

November 23

*The salvation of the righteous
is of the Lord: he is their strength
in the time of trouble.*

PSALM 37:39

Whatever the circumstances,
whatever the call, whatever the duty,
whatever the price,
whatever the sacrifice—
His strength will be your strength
in your hour of need.

February 9

For here have we no continuing city,
but we seek one to come.

HEBREWS 13:14

The power of death has been broken and
death's fear has been removed.
Without the resurrection of Christ there
could be no hope for the future.
The Bible promises that someday we are
going to stand face to face with the
resurrected Christ, and we are going to
have bodies like unto His own body.

November 22

I waited patiently for the Lord;
and he inclined unto me,
and heard my cry.

PSALM 40:1

Effective prayer is offered in faith. If you
want to get your prayers through to God,
surrender your stubborn will to Him,
and He will hear your cry.
Obedience is the master key
to effective prayer.

February 10

*The angel of the Lord encampeth round
about them that fear him,
and delivereth them.*

PSALM 34:7

Every true believer in Christ should be
encouraged and strengthened! Angels are
watching; they mark our path. They
superintend the events of our lives and
protect the interest of the Lord God,
always working to promote His plans and
to bring about his highest will for us.

November 21

*Save thy people,
and bless thine inheritance....*

PSALM 28:9

The family was ordained of God before He
established any other institution,
even before He established the church.
No one is truly a success in God's eyes
if his family is a mess.

February 11

In all these things we are more than conquerors through him who loved us.
ROMANS 8:37, NIV

As a child of God, you need never suffer spiritual defeat. Your days of defeat are over. From now on, you will want to live every minute to its fullest. Every new day will be filled with opportunities to serve others.

November 20

God is our refuge and strength,
an ever present help in trouble.

PSALM 46:1, NIV

If we make our sorrow and trouble an
occasion for learning more of God's love
and of His power to aid and bless,
then it will teach us to have a firmer
confidence in His providence;
and as a result of this, the brightness of
His love will fill our lives.

February 12

Now faith is being sure of what we hope for and certain of what we do not see.

HEBREWS 12:1, NIV

Whether or not we sense and feel the presence of the Holy Spirit or one of the holy angels, by faith we are certain God will never leave us nor forsake us.

November 19

For this God is our God for ever and ever:
he will be our guide even unto death.

PSALM 48:14

God knows us, how we work,
and what is best for us. If we will only
relinquish the controls to Him, He will see
us safely home. What about you?
Who or what is in control of your life?
Are you still holding on to the controls or
have you allowed God to take control yet?
What are you waiting for?

February 13

*By faith Abraham...obeyed and went,
even though he did not know
where he was going.*

HEBREWS 11:8, NIV

The Bible teaches that God does not
always deliver His saints from adversity.
God has not promised to deliver us *from*
trouble, but He has promised to go
with us through the trouble.

November 18

Behold, what manner of love the Father hath bestowed upon us.

1 JOHN 3:1

If God had only talked about how much He loved us and never proved it by sending Christ to meet our greatest need, He would have been a very cruel God. But He demonstrated His love for us by sending the most precious offering He could make: His only and sinless Son.

February 14

By faith Noah, being warned by God concerning events as yet unseen, took heed and constructed an ark for the saving of his household.

HEBREWS 11:7, RSV

While there is life, there is hope.
The Spirit of God is knocking faithfully
at the door. If we repent, mend our ways,
throw off our sins, we can yet be used
of God to bring healing and help
to a dying civilization.

November 17

*Wash me, and I shall be
whiter than snow.*

PSALM 51:7

It is only when our sins have been
washed in the blood of Christ that we
appear white as snow in the eyes of God.
No human "detergent" of good works or
clean thoughts can make us that white,
that pure. Only Christ's precious blood
can do that, and it is only His blood that
can continue to cleanse us from sin.

February 15

His servants shall serve him.

REVELATION 22:3

The Father's house will be a happy home
because there will be work to do there.
Each one will be given exactly the task
that suits his abilities. Perhaps God will
give us new worlds to conquer. Perhaps
He will send us to explore some distant
planet or star, there to preach His
message of everlasting love. Whatever we
do, the Bible says we will serve Him.

November 16

The sacrifice acceptable to God is a broken spirit; a broken and contrite heart, O God, thou wilt not despise.

PSALM 51:17, RSV

Popularity and adulation can be far more dangerous for the Christian than persecution. It is, unfortunately, easy when all goes well to lose our sense of balance and our perspective. We must learn like Paul "how to abound" and "how to be abased."

February 16

You yourselves had {in heaven} better and lasting possessions.

HEBREWS 10:34, NIV

Some time ago two old friends were dying.
The one was rich, and the other poor.
The rich man was outside of Christ, and
he was talking to another of his friends.
"When I die," he said, "I shall have
to leave my riches. When he dies, he
will go to his riches."

November 15

Cast your burden on the Lord, and he will sustain you; he will never permit the righteous to be moved.

PSALM 55:22, RSV

In the middle of our world troubles, the Christian is not to go about wringing his hands, shouting: "What shall we do?" having more nervous tension and worry than anyone else. The Christian is to trust quietly that God is working out things according to His own plan.

February 17

Therefore, since we are surrounded by such a great cloud of witnesses....

HEBREWS 12:1, NIV

Our certainty that angels right now witness how we are walking through life should mightily influence the decisions we make. God is watching, and His angels are interested spectators, too. In the heat of the battle, I have thought how wonderful it would be if we could hear the angels cheering.

November 14

You, O God, tested us; you refined us like silver. You brought us into prison and laid burdens on our backs...we went through fire and water, but you brought us to a place of abundance.

PSALM 66:8-12, NIV

When Jesus Christ is with a person, that one can endure the deepest suffering and somehow emerge a better and stronger Christian because of it.

February 18

*Let us draw near with a true heart
in full assurance of faith.*

HEBREWS 10:22

When you give all you know of yourself to
all that you know of Him, then you can
accept by faith that you are filled with the
Spirit of God. That means that He can
have all of you. Commitment actually is
surrender—total, absolute, unconditional,
irreversible surrender.

November 13

The chariots of God are twenty thousand, even thousands of angels: the Lord is among them, as in Sinai, in the holy place.

PSALM 68:17

Of one thing we can be sure: angels never draw attention to themselves, but ascribe glory to God and press His message upon the hearers as a delivering and sustaining word of the highest order. Believers, look up; take courage. The angels are nearer than you think.

February 19

We have this hope as an anchor of the soul, firm and secure.

HEBREWS 6:19, NIV

For the Christian the fear (of death) is removed. He has the assurance that the sins for which he would be judged at death have been dealt with.

November 12

My strength is made perfect in weakness.

2 CORINTHIANS 12:9

God wants the faith of man
to be placed in Him and not in
human armaments or physical strength.
In our own lives, God wants us to be
broken in spirit so that He can make us
strong at the broken places.

February 20

Peace I leave with you,
my peace I give unto you.

JOHN 14:27

Do you know this peace that only Christ
can give? You can know it today by
repenting of your sins and receiving
Christ as your Lord, Master, and Savior.
And you can do it right now wherever you
are, anywhere in the world.

November 11

We are more than conquerors through him that loved us.

ROMANS 8:37

God wants us to live *victorious* lives, lives that are constantly conquering sin. There is only one way to have victory over sin. That is to be so closely walking with Christ that sin no more abounds in your life, that sin becomes the exception with you rather than the rule as it was before.

February 21

*Blessed is the nation whose
God is the Lord.*

PSALM 33:12, NIV

Today the world is being carried on a
rushing torrent of history that is sweeping
out of control. There is but one power
available to redeem the course of events,
and that is the power of prayer by
God-fearing, Christ-believing people.

November 10

*My soul longs, yea, faints for the
courts of the Lord; my heart and flesh
sing for joy to the living God.*

PSALM 84:2, RSV

We are never more fulfilled
than when our longing for God
is met by His presence in our lives.

February 22

Because he himself suffered when he was tempted, he is able to help those who are being tempted.

HEBREWS 2:18, NIV

Not only are we comforted in our trials, but *our trials can equip us to comfort others.* Our goal should be to learn all we can from what we are called upon to endure, so that we can fulfill a ministry of comfort—as Jesus did.

November 9

O Lord...revive thy work in the midst of the years.

HABAKKUK 3:2

We have not seen a revival in America since shortly after the turn of the twentieth century. But, if we are to see a revival in our nation, it must begin in the hearts of individual believers. What are you doing in your daily walk with God that will bring revival to your life?

February 23

Are they not all ministering spirits sent forth to serve, for the sake of those who are to obtain salvation?

HEBREWS 1:14, RSV

We must be aware that angels keep in close and vital contact with all that is happening on the earth. We must attest to their invisible presence and unceasing labors. Let us believe that they are here among us. We do know they delight with us over every victory in our lives.

November 8

I will hear what God the Lord will say;
For he will speak peace to His people,
to his godly ones.

PSALM 85:8, NASB

Levels of living we have never attained
await us. Peace, satisfaction, and joy we
have never experienced are available to
us. God is trying to break through. The
heavens are calling and God is speaking!

February 24

That being justified by his grace,
we should be made heirs according to the
hope of eternal life.

When I see Christ hanging there,
the spikes in His hands, the crown of
thorns on His brow...I see the picture
of God's grace toward men. I know then
that man cannot work his way to heaven,
and nothing can equal God's infinite
love for sinful men.

November 7

For the Lord knoweth the way of the righteous: but the way of the ungodly shall perish.

PSALM 1:6

All righteousness is rooted in belief. Believe God for all His promises and He will count it unto you as righteousness. Believe on the Lord Jesus Christ, God's ultimate standard and incarnation of righteousness, and be saved.

February 25

*Awaiting our blessed hope, the appearing
of the glory of our great God and
Savior Jesus Christ.*

One of America's best-known columnists
said, "For us all, the world is
disorderly and dangerous; ungoverned,
and apparently ungovernable." The
question arises: Who will restore order?
Who alone can govern the world?
The only answer is Jesus Christ!

November 6

Thou rulest the raging of the sea: when the waves thereof arise, thou stillest them.

PSALM 89:9

This is peace—to be able to sleep in the storm! In Christ, we are relaxed and at peace in the midst of the confusions, bewilderments, and perplexities of this life. The storm rages, but our hearts are at rest.

February 26

When Christ, who is our life,
shall appear, then shall ye also
appear with him in glory.

COLOSSIANS 3:4

One of the best ways to get rid of
discouragement is to remember that
Christ is coming again. The Bible
accurately foretells the future, and
it says that the consummation of
all things shall be the coming again
of Jesus Christ to this earth.

November 5

I will say of the Lord, he is my refuge and my fortress: my God; in him will I trust.

PSALM 91:2

God keeps on giving. He meets our daily physical needs. He delivers us from evil when we stay close to Him.
And there is never a time when we are separated from His care and concern.
How could there be? His Son died for us. Can you think of a better reason why God would care for us?

February 27

*Wherefore seeing we also are
compassed about with so great a
cloud of witnesses....*

HEBREWS 12:1

Our valleys may be filled with foes and
tears; but we can lift our eyes to the hills
to see God and the angels, heaven's
spectators, who support us according
to God's infinite wisdom as they prepare
our welcome home.

November 4

The Son of Man will send out his angels, and they will weed out of his kingdom everything that causes sin and all who do evil. Then the righteous will shine like the sun in the kingdom of their Father.

MATTHEW 13:41,43

You should be preparing to meet Christ, because no one knows the day or the hour when life will end and God's angels, who have been protecting you, will then usher you into the presence of Christ.

February 28

*The effectual fervent prayer of a
righteous man availeth much.*

JAMES 5:16

From one end of the Bible to the other,
there is the record of this plus men who
turned the tide of history by prayer; men
who fervently prayed, and God answered.
The problems of the world will never
be settled unless our national leaders
go to God in prayer.

November 3

For he will give his angels charge of you to guard you in all your ways.

PSALM 91:11, RSV

God has his own secret agents—angels. God's angels never fail in their appointed tasks. We will never know how many potentially fatal accidents were avoided because God's angels protected us.

February 29

*All that will live godly in Christ Jesus
shall suffer persecution.*
2 TIMOTHY 3:12

A Christian's goodness is a rebuke to
another's wickedness; his being
right side up is a reflection upon the
worldling's inverted position. So conflict
is natural. And persecution is inevitable.

November 2

All your sons will be taught by the Lord,
and great will be your children's peace.

ISAIAH 54:13, NIV

For best results in marriage and in
rearing children and building a stable
home, follow the instructions of the One
who performed the first wedding in the
Garden of Eden. Those instructions are in
the Bible. You can have the right kind
of home. Your home can be united
if it is now divided.

March 1

*And the Lord's servant must not be
quarrelsome but kindly to every one,
an apt teacher, forbearing, correcting
his opponents with gentleness.*

2 TIMOTHY 2:24-25, RSV

Jesus was a gentle person. Wherever
true Christianity has gone, His
followers have performed acts of
gentleness and kindness.

November 1

Wait on the Lord: be of good courage,
and he shall strengthen thine heart:
wait, I say, on the Lord.

PSALM 27:14

I have never met a person who spent time
in daily prayer and in the study of God's
Word and who was strong in the faith
who was ever discouraged for very long.
You cannot be discouraged if you are
close to the One who gives all hope and
plenty to be encouraged about.

March 2

Nevertheless, God's solid foundation stands firm, sealed with this inscription: "The Lord knows those who are his."

2 TIMOTHY 2:19, NIV

The Spirit *witnesses* to us by His Word and within our hearts that Christ died for us, and by faith in Him we have become God's children. What a wonderful thing to know the Holy Spirit has been given to us as a seal—a pledge—and a witness!

October 31

God hath from the beginning chosen you.

2 THESSALONIANS 2:13

God thought of *you* even before He made
the world, even before He made you. It is
that God who loves you and longs to have
the deepest and closest relationship
possible with you.

March 3

If we suffer, we shall also reign with him.
2 TIMOTHY 2:12

Life cannot lose its zest when down underneath our present discomfort is the knowledge that we are children of a King. "All things" are taken in stride; burdens become blessings in disguise; every wound, like good surgery, is for our good; and etched in every cross is the symbol of a crown.

October 30

I urge you, brothers, in view of God's mercy, to offer your bodies as living sacrifices, holy and pleasing to God—this is your spiritual act of worship.

ROMANS 12:1, NIV

We have heard the modern expression, "Don't fight it—it's bigger than both of us." Those who submit to the will of God do not fight back at life. They learn the secret of surrender, of yielding to God. He then fights for us!

March 4

I know whom I have believed.
2 TIMOTHY 1:12

All of our difficulties are not solved the moment we are converted to Christ, but conversion does mean that we can approach our problems with a new attitude and in a new strength.

October 29

As for man, his days are as grass:
as a flower of the field,
so he flourisheth.

PSALM 103:15

Our days are filled with tiny golden
minutes with eternity in them. Our lives
are immortal. One thousand years from
this day you will be more alive than you
are at this moment. There is a future life
with God for those who put their trust in
His Son, Jesus Christ.

March 5

For the love of money is the root of all evils; it is through this craving that some have wandered away from the faith.

1 TIMOTHY 6:10, RSV

Materialism has become the god of too many of us. The Bible teaches that preoccupation with material possessions is a form of idolatry. And God hates idolatry. The Bible declares, "What shall it profit a man, if he shall gain the whole world, and lose his own soul?

October 28

I go to prepare a place for you.

JOHN 14:2

When we as Christians die, we go straight into the presence of Christ, straight to that place, straight to that mansion in heaven to spend eternity with God. The place we are going to has an address just as the place in which we are now living has an address. It is a real place.

March 6

We...suffer reproach, because we trust in the living God.

1 TIMOTHY 4:10

The persecuted are happy because they
are being processed for heaven.
Persecution is to the Christian what
"growing pains" are to the growing child.
No pain, no development. No suffering,
no glory. No struggle, no victory.
No persecution, no reward!

October 27

Bless the Lord, ye his angels, that excel in strength, that do his commandments, hearkening unto the voice of his word.

PSALM 103:20

If you are a believer in Christ, expect powerful angels to accompany you in your life experiences. Lord, give me the eyes to see the angels around me.

March 7

I will therefore that men pray every where, lifting up holy hands, without wrath and doubting.

1 TIMOTHY 2:8

Never before in history have we stood in greater need of prayer. Will we be people of prayer for such a time as this?

October 26

Oh that men would praise the Lord for his goodness, and for his wonderful works to the children of men! For he satisfieth the longing soul, and filleth the hungry soul with goodness.

PSALM 107:8-9

This is the secret of soul-satisfaction: Let your soul delight itself in fatness. Remove the obstructions, tear down the barriers, and let your soul find the fulfillment of its deepest longings in fellowship with God.

March 8

For I delivered unto you first of all that which I also received, how that Christ died for our sins according to the scriptures; and that he was buried, and that he rose again the third day.

1 CORINTHIANS 15: 3-4

The work of Christ is a fact, His cross is a fact, His tomb is a fact, His resurrection is a fact. You are not called upon to believe something that is not credible, but to believe in the fact of history.

October 25

My spirit made diligent search.

PSALM 77:6

God is sending forth His message of love,
but we must be on the right wavelength.
We must be willing to receive His message
and then to obey it.

March 9

But when I, the Messiah, shall come in my glory, and all the angels with me, then I shall sit upon my throne of glory.

MATTHEW 25:31, LB

What a moment it is going to be for believers throughout all the ages, from every tribe, nation, and tongue, when they are presented in the Court of Heaven. Scripture calls it, "the marriage supper of the Lamb" (Revelation 19:9).

October 24

*Your word is a lamp to my feet
and a light for my path.*

PSALM 119:105, NIV

The Bible is our one sure guide
in an unsure world. We should begin
the day with the Book, and as it
comes to a close let the Word
speak its wisdom to our souls.

March 10

*May our Lord Jesus Christ himself
and God our Father, who loved us
and by his grace gave us eternal
encouragement and good hope, encourage
your hearts and strengthen you.*

2 THESSALONIANS 2:16-17, NIV

We can look to God as our Father. We can
have a personal sense of His love for us
and His interest in us, for He is
concerned about us as a father is
concerned for his children.

October 23

Your word, O Lord, is eternal;
it stands firm in the heavens.

PSALM 119:89, NIV

The Bible has survived every scratch of
human pen. It has survived the assault of
skeptics, agnostics, and atheists. It has
never been proved wrong by a single
archaeological discovery. It remains
supreme in its revelation of redemption.
God still speaks to us today through that
same Word, which stands forever.

March 11

When he putteth forth his own sheep,
he goeth before them, and the sheep
follow him: for they know his voice.

JOHN 10:4

Whatever awaits us is *encountered* first by
Him—like the oriental shepherd always
went ahead of his sheep—therefore any
attack on sheep has to *deal first* with the
shepherd—all the *tomorrows* of our lives
have to pass Him before they get to us!

October 22

I lift up my eyes to the hills.
From whence does my help come?
My help comes from the Lord,
who made heaven and earth.

PSALM 121:1-2, RSV

As we look unto God instead of at ourselves and our circumstances, our perspectives change. Do not be bogged down in the circumstances of life. Look unto the hills for the guidance of Christ.

March 12

He will wipe every tear from their eyes. There will be no more death or mourning or crying or pain.

REVELATION 21:4, NIV

Christ at His return will take away suffering; He says He will wipe away all tears. There will be no more backaches or headaches; cancer and heart disease will be eliminated; mental illness will be no more. All the diseases of mankind will be cured when Christ comes back.

October 21

Except the Lord build the house,
they labor in vain that build it:
except the Lord keep the city,
the watchman waketh but in vain.

PSALM 127:1

Only what is built on the solid foundation
of Christ will last. As the poem says,
"Only one life, 'twill soon be past.
Only what's done for Christ shall last."

March 13

And the very God of peace sanctify you wholly; and I pray God your whole spirit and soul and body be preserved blameless unto the coming of our Lord Jesus Christ.

1 THESSALONIANS 5:23

God is first of all concerned with what you are. What you do is the result of what you are.

October 20

*God's love has been poured into our
hearts through the Holy Spirit
which has been given to us.*

ROMANS 5:5, RSV

The moment I receive Jesus Christ as
Savior, the Holy Spirit takes up residence
in my heart. For the Christian to grow in
wisdom and knowledge of the Word of
God, he must be willing to study God's
Word and to be a willing pupil of
God's Holy Spirit.

March 14

Pray without ceasing.
1 THESSALONIANS 5:17

Try to have a systematic method of
prayer. The devil will fight you every
step of the way. There will be many
interruptions, but keep at it! Don't be
discouraged. Soon you will find that these
periods of prayer are the greatest delight
in your life. You will look forward
to them with more anticipation than
to anything else.

October 19

I have set before you life and death...
therefore choose life,
that you and your descendants may live.

DEUTERONOMY 30:19, RSV

There are eternal benefits that come
from making the right choice.
There are also eternal consequences
for making the wrong choice.
Which choices have you been
making in your life?

March 15

For yourselves know perfectly that
the day of the Lord so cometh as
a thief in the night.

1 THESSALONIANS 5:2

Readiness and watchfulness are all urged
upon Christians, lest Christ's coming,
taking us by surprise, should
find us unprepared.

October 18

*Search me, O God, and know my heart!
Try me and know my thoughts! And see if
there be any wicked way in me, and lead
me in the way everlasting.*

PSALM 139:23-24, RSV

Unless God is revealed to us through
personal experience, we can never really
know God. Most of us know *about* God,
but that is quite different from really
knowing God.

March 16

To them God has chosen to make known among the Gentiles the glorious riches of this mystery, which is Christ in you, the hope of glory.

COLOSSIANS 1:27, NIV

There is one great fact which gives the Christian assurance in the face of death: the *resurrection of Jesus Christ.* It is the physical, bodily resurrection of Christ that gives us confidence and hope.

October 17

The Lord is nigh unto all them that call upon him, to all that call upon him in truth.

PSALM 145:18

Suffering teaches us *patience.*
These words were found penned on the wall of a prison cell in Europe:
"I believe in the sun even when it is not shining. I believe in love even when I don't feel it. I believe in God even when He is silent."

March 17

*For in him all the fulness of God was
pleased to dwell, and through him to
reconcile to himself all things,
whether on earth or in heaven, making
peace by the blood of his cross.*

COLOSSIANS 1:19-20, RSV

In an infinite way that staggers our hearts
and minds, we know that Christ paid the
penalty for our sins, past, present, and
future. That is why He died on the cross.

October 16

The Lord loveth the righteous.

PSALM 146:8

Based upon what we do know about God's character, demonstrated supremely in the Cross, we can trust that God is doing what is best for our lives. As Corrie ten Boom once explained, "Picture a piece of embroidery placed between you and God, with the right side up toward God. Man sees the loose, frayed ends; but God sees the pattern."

March 18

The Lord hath laid on him
the iniquity of us all.

ISAIAH 53:6

God said from the cross: "I love you."
He was also saying: "I can forgive you."
God in Christ had a basis for forgiveness.
Because Christ died, God can justify the
sinner and still be just. The cross is
God's great plus sign of history.

October 15

Great is our Lord, and of great power:
his understanding is infinite.

PSALM 147:5

God's love is unchangeable. He loves us
in spite of knowing us as we really are.
Were it not for the love of God,
none of us would ever have a chance.

March 19

My God will meet all your needs according to his glorious riches in Christ Jesus.

PHILIPPIANS 4:19, NIV

Many times we make the mistake of thinking that Christ's help is needed only for sickrooms or in times of overwhelming sorrow and suffering. This is not true. Jesus wishes to enter into every mood and every moment of our lives. I do not believe that anything happens to the obedient Christian by accident.

October 14

Pride goeth before destruction, and a haughty spirit before a fall.

PROVERBS 16:18

A nation can rise no higher, can be no stronger, and be no better than the individuals which compose that nation! David realized this truth; and in wisdom, he concluded that he should start making things right in *himself*! Each one of us needs to reach that same conclusion.

March 20

I can do all things through
Christ which strengtheneth me.

PHILIPPIANS 4:13

The moment you come to Christ, the
Spirit of God brings the life of God into
you and you begin to live. There's a whole
new direction to your life because the
Spirit of God has given to you the very life
of God, and God is an eternal God—that
means you'll live as long as God lives.

October 13

But happy is the man who has the God of Jacob as his helper, whose hope is in the Lord his God.

PSALM 146:5, TLB

True happiness begins when one is in a right relationship with God. God is the only source of true happiness, because He offers those intangibles: contentment, security, peace, and hope for the future.

March 21

Fret not thyself....
PSALM 37:1

Anticipation of trouble makes trifles
appear unduly large, and the troubles
that never come make up an imagined
burden that will crush the spirit. They are
haunting specters, as unsubstantial as a
bad dream, and we spend the strength
that should be expended in constructive
work and services in fighting problems
that do not even exist.

October 12

Train up a child in the way he should go:
and when he is old,
he will not depart from it.

PROVERBS 22:6

The majority of children acquire the
characteristics and habits of their
parents. What are they learning from us?

March 22

Have no anxiety about anything,
but in everything by prayer and
supplication with thanksgiving let your
requests be made known to God.

PHILIPPIANS 4:6, RSV

Happy is the person who has learned the
secret of coming to God daily in prayer.
Fifteen minutes alone with God every
morning can change our outlooks and
recharge our batteries.

October 11

Give, and it will be given to you. A good measure, pressed down, shaken together and running over, will be poured into your lap. For with the measure you use, it will be measured to you.

LUKE 6:38, NIV

Giving to God is a guaranteed investment with a certain return. God wants us to be a channel of blessing to others. When we are, it is we who receive the greatest blessing of all.

March 23

Rejoice in the Lord always.
I will say it again: Rejoice!

PHILIPPIANS 4:4, NIV

Resentment or resignation are not the
answer to the problem of suffering.
And there is a step beyond mere
acceptance. It is *accepting with joy.*
The Christian life is a joyful life.
The ability to rejoice in any situation
is a sign of spiritual maturity.

October 10

Holy, holy, holy, is the Lord of hosts.

ISAIAH 6:3

Christ cried out on the cross, "My God, my God, why hast thou forsaken me?" What a terribly frightening and horrible moment that was, as the blackness of man's sin caused the Father to turn away in disgust. Yet what a glorious moment it was, as Christ took upon His holy and sinless self all of the penalty that should be ours because of our sinfulness.

March 24

I count all things but loss for the excellency of the knowledge of Christ Jesus my Lord.

PHILIPPIANS 3:8

Christians can rejoice in the midst of persecution because they have eternity's values in view. The thought of the future life with its prerogatives and joys helps to make the trials of the present seem light and transient. "...for theirs is the kingdom of heaven."

October 9

I am the resurrection, and the life:
he that believeth in me, though he were
dead, yet shall he live.

JOHN 11:25

The Christian should never consider
death a tragedy. Rather he should see it
as the angels do: they realize that joy
should mark the journey from time to
eternity. The way to life is by the valley of
death, but the road is marked with victory
all the way.

March 25

And being found in fashion as a man, he humbled himself, and became obedient unto death, even the death of the cross.

PHILIPPIANS 2:8

The cross presents itself in the midst of our dilemma as our only hope.
Here is power enough to transform human nature. Here is power enough to change the world.

October 8

He will swallow up death forever,
and the Lord God will wipe away tears
from all faces.

ISAIAH 25:8, RSV

Victor Hugo said of death: "When I go
down to the grave I can say, like so many
others: I have finished my work, but I
cannot say I have finished my life. My
day's work will begin the next morning.
My tomb closes in the twilight to be
opened in the dawn."

March 26

Let this mind be in you,
which was also in Christ Jesus.

PHILIPPIANS 2:5

We Christians are not to be conformed to
this world mentally. We are not even to be
conformed to the world's anxieties. We are
to be lights in the midst of darkness, and
our lives should exemplify relaxation,
peace, and joy in the midst of frustration,
confusion, and despair.

October 7

Casting all your care upon him;
for he careth for you.

1 PETER 5:7

God has taken the responsibility for our
care and worry. You can be positively
assured that God does care for you, and if
God cares for you and has promised to
carry your burdens and cares, then
nothing should distress you.

March 27

If ye suffer for
righteousness' sake, happy are ye.

1 PETER 3:14

Sometimes it takes suffering to make us
realize the brevity of life, and the
importance of living for Christ.
Often God uses suffering to accomplish
things in our lives that would
otherwise never be achieved.

October 6

He tends his flock like a shepherd:
He gathers the lambs in his arms and
carries them close to his heart.

ISAIAH 40:11, NIV

Jesus the Good Shepherd *owns* the sheep: they belong to Him. He *guards* the sheep: He never abandons them when danger is near. He *knows* them each by name and leads them out. And He *lays down his life* for the sheep; such is the measure of His love.

March 28

For it has been granted to you that for the sake of Christ you should not only believe in him but also suffer for his sake.

PHILIPPIANS 1:29, RSV

If you are physically well, praise God and learn not to complain about comparably minor irritations. If you do suffer from a physical infirmity, remember that the Lord is your strength and He will not only see you through this life, but He will give you a brand new body in the next life.

October 5

Fear thou not; for I am with thee:
be not dismayed; for I am thy God:
I will strengthen thee; yea, I will help thee;
yea, I will uphold thee with the right hand
of my righteousness.

ISAIAH 41:10

How many times do you and I fret and turn, looking for a little peace? God's peace can be in our hearts—right now. Ask for God's peace and see what a transformation will take place in your life.

March 29

For me to live is Christ, and to die is gain.
PHILIPPIANS 1:21

Jesus Christ said: "I am the resurrection,
and the life: he that believeth in me,
though he were dead, yet shall he live:
and whosoever liveth and believeth in me
shall never die" (John 11:25-26).
Our hope of immortality is based on
Christ alone.

October 4

See, I have refined you, though not as silver; I have tested you in the furnace of affliction.

ISAIAH 48:10, NIV

When Job had lost everything he did not say, "The Lord gave and the devil has taken away," but "The Lord gave and the Lord has *taken* away; may the name of the Lord be praised." So when we are hurt, it is important to remember that God Himself has allowed it for a purpose.

March 30

Teach me to do thy will.

PSALM 143:10

One of the most thrilling things about
studying the Bible is to know that the
infinite God has been pleased to share
some of the secrets of His universe
with His redeemed children. And what is
God's will for us today? To know and
to follow the will of God.

October 3

For the Lord comforts his people and will have compassion on his afflicted ones.

ISAIAH 49:13, NIV

Comfort and prosperity have never enriched the world as adversity has done. Out of pain and problems have come the sweetest songs, the most poignant poems, the most gripping stories. Out of suffering and tears have come the greatest spirits and the most blessed lives.

March 31

Do not get drunk on wine.... Instead,
be filled with the Spirit.

EPHESIANS 5:18, NIV

We are not filled (with the Spirit)
once for all, like a bucket. Instead,
we are to be filled constantly. The
Christian is...constantly to accept the
direction and energy of the Spirit
so he is always overflowing.

October 2

The fool hath said in his heart,
There is no God.

PSALM 14:1

We receive only one life during which we
have many chances to come to know God.
We are the biggest fools of all if we make
the eternal mistake of rejecting the truth
that God has communicated to us.

April 1

Lo, I am with you alway,
even unto the end of the world.

MATTHEW 28:20

We may claim this promise from our
Savior and Lord. He *does* go with us
through our sufferings, and He awaits us
as we emerge on the other side of the
tunnel of testing—into the light of His
glorious presence to live with Him forever!

October 1

For we know that if our earthly house of this tabernacle were dissolved, we have a building of God, an house not made with hands, eternal in the heavens.

2 CORINTHIANS 5:1

After becoming a Christian, all of our life becomes a preparation for our journey to heaven. Are you going to heaven? Have you started packing yet?

April 2

Be renewed in the spirit of your minds,
and put on the new nature,
created after the likeness of God in true
righteousness and holiness.

EPHESIANS 4:23-24, RSV

There are thousands of people who do not give themselves to Jesus Christ, because they have conformed to the world. A true Christian does not conform himself to the worldly concepts of religion. Instead, he is to become a true "follower" of the Lord.

September 30

"Don't be alarmed," he said. "You are looking for Jesus the Nazarene, who was crucified. He has risen! He is not here."

MARK 16:6, NIV

Easter has been popularized and commercialized by merchants and the secular establishment. But the message of Easter is the central focus of Christianity. What does Easter mean to you? It means to me that Christ is risen!

April 3

No discipline seems pleasant at the time, but painful. Later on, however, it produces a harvest of righteousness and peace for those who have been trained by it.

HEBREWS 12:11, NIV

To resent and resist God's disciplining hand is to miss one of the greatest spiritual blessings we Christians can enjoy this side of heaven.

September 29

God hath both raised up the Lord, and will
also raise up us by his own power.

1 Corinthians 6:14

If you trust the resurrected Christ
as your Lord and Savior, He will be with
you when you die, and will give you life
with Him forever.

April 4

That Christ may dwell in your hearts through faith; that you, being rooted and grounded in love, may...know the love of Christ which surpasses knowledge.

EPHESIANS 3:17-19, RSV

God possesses infinite knowledge and an awareness which is uniquely His. At all times, even in the midst of any type of suffering, I can realize that He knows, loves, watches, understands, and more than that, He has a purpose.

September 28

Therefore shall a man leave his father and his mother, and shall cleave unto his wife: and they shall be one flesh.

GENESIS 2:24

Put Christ first in your life and then first in your marriage and you will have a bond between yourself, your mate, and the Lord that no one can break.

April 5

For he is our peace, who hath made both one, and hath broken down the middle wall of partition between us.

EPHESIANS 2:14

The only human hope for peace lies
at the cross of Christ, where all men,
whatever their nationality or race,
can become a new brotherhood.

September 27

The Lord is coming with fire,
and his chariots are like a whirlwind;
he will bring down his anger with fury,
and his rebuke with flames of fire.

ISAIAH 66:15, NIV

What would you do differently if you knew
He was coming today?

April 6

But now in Christ Jesus you who once were far off have been brought near in the blood of Christ.

EPHESIANS 2:13, RSV

God is saying to the whole world, "I love you. I am willing to forgive your sins." God is saying to all those who are lonely today, "Behold, I am with you until the end of the age" (cf. Matthew 28:20).

September 26

God hath chosen the foolish things of the world to confound the wise; and God hath chosen the weak things of the world to confound the things which are mighty.

1 CORINTHIANS 1:27

The Bible says there are two kinds of wisdom in the world. First, there is wisdom that is given by God, a wisdom which views life in terms of eternity. The second is the wisdom of the world. Which kind of wisdom will you choose?

April 7

For we are his workmanship,
created in Christ Jesus unto good works,
which God hath before ordained that
we should walk in them.

EPHESIANS 2:10

The man who has experienced the new
birth is a member of God's household. His
will is changed, his objectives for living
are changed, his disposition is changed,
his affections are changed, and he now
has purpose and meaning in his life.

September 25

Blessed is the man that trusteth in the Lord, and whose hope the Lord is.

JEREMIAH 17:7

The hope we have in Christ is an absolute certainty. We can be sure that the place Christ is preparing for us will be ready when we arrive, because with Him nothing is left to chance. Everything He promised He will deliver.

April 8

For by grace are ye saved through faith;
and that not of yourselves:
it is the gift of God: not of works,
lest any man should boast.

EPHESIANS 2:8-9

The grace is God's: the faith is ours.
God gave us the free will with which to
choose. God gave us the capacity to
believe and trust.

September 24

I have loved thee with an everlasting love: therefore with lovingkindness have I drawn thee.

JEREMIAH 31:3

It was love that enabled Jesus Christ to become poor that we through His poverty might be rich.

April 9

I pray not that thou shouldest take them out of the world, but that thou shouldest keep them from the evil.

JOHN 17:15

God has provided us the power to resist the world and be separated from it, and it is ours to appropriate that power every hour of our lives. We are in the world, but the world is not to be in us.

September 23

For the preaching of the cross is to them that perish foolishness; but unto us who are saved it is the power of God.

1 CORINTHIANS 1:18

No sin has been committed in the world today that can compare with the full cup of the universe's sin that brought Jesus to the cross. To you, sin may be a small thing; to God, it is a great and awful thing. It is the second largest thing in the world; only the love of God is greater.

April 10

But God forbid that I should glory,
save in the cross of our Lord Jesus Christ,
by whom the world is crucified unto me,
and I unto the world.

GALATIANS 6:14

Wherever you are at this moment,
yield your life unconditionally to God,
and He can still make it a thing
of beauty and an honor to His name.

September 22

For I will forgive their iniquity, and I will remember their sin no more.

JEREMIAH 31:34

The God of grace forgets our sins and wipes them completely from His memory forever! He places us in His sight as though we had never committed one sin. It is as if an accounting entry has been made in the books of heaven and the Divine Bookkeeper cancels our debt!

April 11

The fruit of the Spirit is love, joy, peace, longsuffering, gentleness, goodness, faith, meekness, temperance.

GALATIANS 5:22-23

As a Christian you have the will-power to yield either to the flesh and live a fleshly, carnal life; or you have the power to yield to the Spirit, to live a Spirit-filled life. God meant the Christian life to be on the highest possible plane at all times, bearing the fruit of the Spirit.

September 21

I will give them a new heart and a new mind. I will take away their stubborn heart of stone and will give them an obedient heart.

EZEKIEL 11:19, TEV

When a man comes in contact with God, He can never be the same again. God takes the weak and makes them strong, the vile and makes them clean, the worthless and makes them worthwhile, the sinful and makes them sinless.

April 12

The fruit of the Spirit is...peace.
GALATIANS 5:22

Peace carries with it the idea of unity,
completeness, rest, ease, and security.
When you and I yield to worry, we deny
our Guide the right to lead us in
confidence and peace. Only the Holy
Spirit can give us peace in the midst of
the storms of restlessness and despair.

September 20

I will both lay me down in peace, and sleep: for thou, Lord, only makest me dwell in safety.

PSALM 4:8

The next time you have difficulty falling asleep at night (and even when you don't), read from the Psalms. Pick a quiet time in your house and a quiet place and let God soothe your troubled spirit to a point where you receive His rest and you place your trust and confidence in Him.

April 13

This I say then, Walk in the Spirit, and ye shall not fulfil the lust of the flesh.

GALATIANS 5:16

Living for Christ is a day-to-day walking with Him. It is a continuous dependence upon the Spirit of God. It is believing in His faithfulness. If we look to our own resources, our own strength, or our own ability as Peter did when he walked on the water, we will fail.

September 19

Do not love the world or anything in the world. If anyone loves the world, the love of the Father is not in him.

1 JOHN 2:15, NIV

The call of Christ is for rededication to
Him—a call to follow Him,
to pattern our lives after His.
As John Wesley so wisely wrote:
"Anything that cools my love for Christ is
of the world."

April 14

All the law is fulfilled in one word,
even in this; Thou shalt love
thy neighbour as thyself.

GALATIANS 5:14

Without Jesus Christ in your heart, you
can't have this love. You can't produce
this love except with the power of the Holy
Spirit. That's the reason you must receive
Christ, and when you do, He gives you
the power and the strength, through the
Holy Spirit, to produce this love.

September 18

*I beseech you therefore, brethren,
by the mercies of God, that ye present
your bodies a living sacrifice, holy,
acceptable unto God, which is your
reasonable service.*

ROMANS 12:1

We owe God everything!
We have been bought and paid for with a
terrible price, the broken body and shed
blood of God's Son.

April 15

*We through the Spirit wait for the hope
of righteousness by faith.*

GALATIANS 5:5

In the midst of the pessimism, gloom, and
frustration of the present hour there is
one bright beacon light of hope—and that
is the promise of Jesus Christ, "If I go
and prepare a place for you, I will
come again" [John 14:3].

September 17

Then Daniel said unto the king...My God hath sent his angel, and hath shut the lions' mouths, that they have not hurt me.

DANIEL 6:21-22

Angels minister to us personally. We may not always be aware of the presence of angels. We can't always predict how they will appear. But angels have been said to be our neighbors. Often they may be our companions without our being aware of their presence.

April 16

For ye are all the children of God
by faith in Christ Jesus.

GALATIANS 3:26

Because God is responsible for our
welfare, we are told to cast all our
care upon Him, for He cares for us
(I Peter 5:7). God says, "I'll take the
burden—don't give it a thought—leave it
to me." God is keenly aware that we are
dependent upon Him for life's necessities.

September 16

There was a violent earthquake, for an angel of the Lord came down from heaven and, going to the tomb, rolled back the stone and sat on it.

MATTHEW 28:2, NIV

No words of men or angels can adequately describe the height and depth, the length and breadth of the glory to which the world awakened when Jesus came forth to life from the pall of death.

April 17

I am crucified with Christ: nevertheless I live: yet not I, but Christ liveth in me: and the life which I now live in the flesh I live by faith of the Son of God, who loved me, and gave himself for me.

GALATIANS 2:20

Irenaeus said it well when he wrote, "The Word of God, Jesus Christ, on account of His great love for mankind, became what we are in order to make us what he is himself."

September 15

God hath both raised up the Lord, and will also raise up us by his own power.

1 CORINTHIANS 6:14

The Scripture teaches that as Christians, our bodies may go to the grave but they are going to be raised on the great resurrection morning. Then will death be swallowed up in victory. As a result of the resurrection of Christ, the sting of death is gone.

April 18

Who gave himself for our sins, that he might deliver us from this present evil world, according to the will of God and our Father.

GALATIANS 1:4

Evil is present to control and deceive us. We are not at peace with ourselves or with God. That is what the Cross of Christ is all about: to reconcile us to God and to give us a new nature.

September 14

And the angel answered and said unto the women, Fear not ye: for I know that ye seek Jesus, which was crucified. He is not here: for he is risen, as he said.

MATTHEW 28:5-6

One of the angels who was sitting outside the tomb proclaimed the greatest message the world has ever heard: "He is not here: for he is risen." Darkness and despair died; hope and anticipation were born in the hearts of men.

April 19

The grace of the Lord Jesus Christ, and the love of God, and the communion of the Holy Ghost, be with you all.

2 CORINTHIANS 13:14

The Holy Spirit knows everything that we do—He watches us. "His eye is on the sparrow," and if God the Spirit is watching the sparrow, how much more He is watching us every moment.

September 13

Break up your fallow ground, for it is the time to seek the Lord, that he may come and rain salvation upon you.

HOSEA 10:12, RSV

The world problems are big, but God is bigger! If we will dare to take God into account, confess our sin, and rely unreservedly upon Him for wisdom, guidance, and strength, our world problems can yet be solved.

April 20

Except ye be converted, and become as little children, ye shall not enter into the kingdom of heaven.

MATTHEW 18:3

No one can be converted except with the consent of his own free will, because God does not override human choice. God helps a man when he takes the leap.

September 12

Though he were a Son, yet learned he obedience by the things which he suffered; and being made perfect, he became the author of salvation unto all them that obey him.

HEBREWS 5:8-9

In our sufferings and tribulations Jesus Himself must be our chief consideration. We must fix our eyes upon Him. He who suffered for us shows us how we are to bear our sufferings.

April 21

Everyone who wants to live a godly life in Christ Jesus will be persecuted.

2 TIMOTHY 3:12, NIV

It is not easy to be Christ's true follower. As someone has said, "Salvation is *free* but not cheap."

September 11

Turn ye even to me with all your heart...with weeping, and with mourning.

JOEL 2:12

True repentance is a turning from sin—a conscious, deliberate decision to leave sin behind—and a conscious turning to God with a commitment to follow His will for our lives. It is a change of direction, an alteration of attitudes, and a yielding of the will.

April 22

*Thanks be to God
for his indescribable gift!*

2 CORINTHIANS 9:15, NIV

God sent His only Son into the world to die for our sins, so that we might be forgiven. This is a gift for us—God's gift of salvation. This gift is a permanent legacy for everyone who truly admits he has sinned. It is for everyone who reaches out and accepts God's gift by receiving Jesus Christ as his Lord and Savior.

September 10

I will pour out my spirit upon all flesh.

JOEL 2:28

In her book, *The Christian's Secret of a Happy Life*, Hannah Whitall Smith tells us: "...what we need is to see that God's presence is a certain fact always, and that every act of our soul is done right before Him, and that a word spoken in prayer is really spoken to Him, as if our eyes could see Him and our hands could touch Him..."

April 23

Sorrowful, yet always rejoicing;
poor, yet making many rich; having
nothing, and yet possessing everything.

2 CORINTHIANS 6:10, NIV

When was the last time you praised God
in the midst of despair? Don't wait until
you "feel like it" or you'll never do it.
Do it, and then you'll feel like it!

September 9

The Lord will be the hope of his people,
and the strength of the children of Israel.

JOEL 3:16

Upon the authority of God's Word,
I declare that Christ is the answer to
every baffling perplexity which plagues
mankind. In Him is found the cure for
care, a balm for bereavement, a healing
for our hurts, and a sufficiency for
our insufficiency.

April 24

*For he hath made him to be sin for us,
who knew no sin; that we might be made
the righteousness of God in him.*

2 CORINTHIANS 5:21

Christ took our sins. He finished the work
of redemption. I am not saved through
any works or merit of my own. If we are
believers in Jesus Christ, we have already
come through the storm of judgment. It
happened at the cross.

September 8

Ask ye of the Lord rain in the time of the latter rain; so the Lord shall make bright clouds, and give them showers of rain, to every one grass in the field.

ZECHARIAH 10:1

When faced with the clouds of defeat we need to open our hearts and let Him in. Let Him take the clouds of sin out and transform you into a new creature.

April 25

Stir up the gift of God which is in you.

2 TIMOTHY 1:6, NKJV

Every person has been given a gift from God. You may be a farmer, or a laborer, or a doctor, or a professor, but you have been given a gift of the Holy Spirit. (What is your gift?) Each of us is to put his gift into action for God.

September 7

*So when this corruptible shall have put on
incorruption, and this mortal shall have
put on immortality, then shall be brought
to pass the saying that is written,
Death is swallowed up in victory.*

1 CORINTHIANS 15:54

Death is robbed of much of its terror for
the true believer, but we still need God's
protection as we take that last journey.

April 26

I will take away the stony heart...and I will give you an heart of flesh.

EZEKIEL 36:26

It is utterly impossible for me to change my disposition in my own strength. The new birth is something that must be done for me by another; and God has promised to do that which I cannot do for myself. And He will do it for you, too!

September 6

For where your treasure is,
there will your heart be also.

MATTHEW 6:21

Only those who are poor in spirit and rich toward God shall be accounted worthy to enter there, because they come not in their own merit but in the righteousness of the Redeemer. Where is your treasure? In the bank? In the driveway? In the mirror? Or are you storing up your treasure in heaven?

April 27

Old things are passed away;
behold, all things are become new.

2 CORINTHIANS 5:17

So man—distressed, discouraged, unhappy, ruled by selfishness, quarrelsome, confused, depressed, miserable, taking alcohol and barbiturates, looking for escapisms—can come to Christ by faith and emerge a new man. This sounds incredible and yet it is precisely what the Bible teaches.

September 5

Blessed are the meek:
for they shall inherit the earth.

MATTHEW 5:5

It is our human nature to be proud,
not meek. Only the Spirit of God can
transform our lives through the new birth
experience and then make us over again
into the image of Christ, our example of
what pleases God in the way of meekness.

April 28

For our light affliction, which is but for a moment, worketh for us a far more exceeding and eternal weight of glory.

2 CORINTHIANS 4:17

In the last essay he wrote before he died, great Christian apologist C. S. Lewis said, "We have no right to happiness; only an obligation to do our duty." Of course it is in our duty that happiness comes.

September 4

Blessed are the pure in heart:
for they shall see God.

MATTHEW 5:8

Christ provided the possibility of purity by
His death on the cross. The righteousness
and the purity of God are imputed to men
who confess their sins and receive Christ
into their hearts.

April 29

We are afflicted in every way, but not crushed; perplexed, but not driven to despair; persecuted, but not forsaken; struck down, but not destroyed; always carrying in the body the death of Jesus, so that the life of Jesus may also be manifested in our bodies.

2 CORINTHIANS 4:8-10, RSV

Those who keep heaven in view remain serene and cheerful in the darkest day.

September 3

Blessed are the peacemakers:
for they shall be called the
children of God.

MATTHEW 5:9

If we have peace *with* God and the
peace *of* God, we will become
peacemakers.
We will not only be at peace with our
neighbors, but we will be leading
them to discover the source of true
peace in Christ.

April 30

For he is faithful that promised.

HEBREWS 10:23

God has made some incredible promises
to us. He has promised that we might
have a relationship with Him through His
Son. He has promised never to leave us....
Because of God's deposit on our lives,
He is obligated to meet His promises.
And so He has. And so He will.

September 2

Blessed are they which are persecuted for righteousness' sake: for theirs is the kingdom of heaven.

MATTHEW 5:10

Think about it. Have you ever been persecuted for sharing your faith in Christ? Has your faith cost you anything? If not, perhaps you had better re-examine your faith.

May 1

Yea, though I walk through the valley of the shadow of death, I will fear no evil: for thou art with me.

PSALM 23:4

When a loved one dies, it is natural for us to feel a sense of loss and even a deep loneliness. That will not necessarily vanish overnight. But even when we feel the pain of bereavement most intensely, we can also know the gracious and loving presence of Christ most closely.

September 1

Faith without works is dead.

JAMES 2:20

Works are not ends in themselves, but
they demonstrate God's love toward
others so that they will know God loves
them and so that they will desire to
learn about God's provision for their
greatest needs.

May 2

Blessed be the God and Father of our Lord Jesus Christ, the Father of mercies and God of all comfort, who comforts us in all our affliction, so that we may be able to comfort those who are in any affliction.

2 CORINTHIANS 1:3-4, RSV

There are countless opportunities to comfort others, not only in the loss of a loved one, but also in the daily distress that so often creeps into our lives.

August 31

But I say to you, love your enemies and
pray for those who persecute you.

MATTHEW 5:44, RSV

Those who are persecuted for
"righteousness' sake" are happy
because they are identified with Christ.
The enmity of the world is tangible proof
that we are on the right side, that we are
identified with our blessed Lord.

May 3

Thanks be to God, who gives us the victory through our Lord Jesus Christ.

1 CORINTHIANS 15:57, RSV

Victory is yours. Claim it! This doesn't mean the Christian can never suffer defeat or experience low periods in life. But it does mean that the Savior goes with you no matter the problem.

August 30

*And she brought forth her firstborn son,
and wrapped him in swaddling clothes,
and laid him in a manger; because there
was no room for them in the inn.*

LUKE 2:7

Things have not really changed since that
Bethlehem night two thousand years ago.
God is still on the fringes of most of our
lives. Are we in danger, in all of our busy
activities, of excluding from our hearts
and lives the One who made us?

May 4

When the perishable has been clothed with the imperishable, and the mortal with immortality, then the saying that is written will come true: "Death has been swallowed up in victory."

1 CORINTHIANS 15:54, NIV

Once we have reached heaven, we will no longer be troubled or inhibited by physical or bodily limitations.
The crippled, diseased, wasted bodies will be strong and beautiful and vigorous.

August 29

Take heed that ye do not your alms before men, to be seen of them.... But when thou doest alms, let not thy left hand know what thy right hand doeth.

MATTHEW 6:1,3

If a person gets his attitude toward money straight, it will help straighten out almost every other area of his life. The chief motive of the selfish, unregenerate person is "get." The chief motive of the dedicated Christian should be "give."

May 5

Lo! I tell you a mystery. We shall not all sleep, but we shall all be changed.

1 CORINTHIANS 15:51, RSV

As we trust Christ to save us, we can be comforted in the knowledge that He waits on the other side to take our hand and welcome us into His (and our) dwelling place where the mansion He has prepared for us stands in readiness.

August 28

*But lay up for yourselves treasures
in heaven, where neither moth nor rust
consumes and where thieves do not
break in and steal.*

MATTHEW 6:20, RSV

Living a holy life, leading others to Christ
as we share our faith, doing good works
in Christ's name, all of these things are
materials that may be sent on ahead.

May 6

*The last enemy
that shall be destroyed is death.*

1 CORINTHIANS 15:26

Death marks the beginning, not the end.
It is a solemn, dramatic step in our
journey to God.

August 27

Ye cannot serve God and mammon.

MATTHEW 6:24

We have the power to choose whom we
will serve, but the alternative to choosing
Christ brings certain destruction.
Christ said that! The broad, wide,
easy, popular way leads to death and
destruction. Only the way of
the Cross leads home.

May 7

For we know in part and we prophecy in part, but when perfection comes, the imperfect disappears.

1 CORINTHIANS 13:9-10, NIV

Paul believed in Christ and committed his all to Christ. The result was that he *knew* Christ was able to keep him forever. Strong faith and living hope are the result of unconditional commitment to Jesus Christ.

August 26

Therefore do not be anxious, saying, 'What shall we eat?' or 'What shall we drink?' or 'What shall we wear?'

MATTHEW 6:31, RSV

We were never meant to be crushed under the weight of care. We push the button of faith or pull the lever of trust, and our burden is discharged upon the shoulder of Him who said He would gladly bear it.

May 8

Moreover it is required in stewards,
that a man be found faithful.

1 CORINTHIANS 4:2

We Christians should stand out like a
sparkling diamond against a rough and
dark background. We should be poised,
cultured, courteous, gracious, but firm
in the things we do or do not do. We
should laugh and be radiant; but we
should refuse to allow the world to
pull us down to its level.

August 25

But seek ye first the kingdom of God, and his righteousness; and all these things shall be added unto you.

MATTHEW 6:33

I don't believe any world leader will write the last chapter of history—God will write it. I believe...that there is a destiny for the human race far beyond anything we can dream. But it will be God's kingdom and will come in God's way.

May 9

I myself am convinced, my brothers, that you yourselves are full of goodness, complete in knowledge and competent to instruct one another.

ROMANS 15:14, NIV

The immortal John Wesley gave us a goal for goodness: "Do all the good you can, by all the means you can, in all the ways you can, in all the places you can, at all the times you can, to all the people you can, as long as ever you can."

August 24

They gave themselves first to the Lord and then to us in keeping with God's will.

2 CORINTHIANS 8:5, NIV

Only God Himself fully appreciates the influence of a Christian mother in the molding of character in her children. Every mother owes it to her children to accept Christ as her personal Savior, that she may be the influence for good in the lives of those whom Christ has graciously given to her.

May 10

Now the God of hope fill you with all joy and peace in believing, that ye may abound in hope, through the power of the Holy Ghost.

ROMANS 15:13

When faith is strong, troubles become trifles. There can be comfort in sorrow *because in the midst of mourning, God gives a song.*

August 23

Ask, and it will be given you; seek, and you will find; knock, and it will be opened to you. For every one who asks receives, and he who seeks finds, and to him who knocks it will be opened.

MATTHEW 7:7, RSV

God has a particular responsibility to his children; Oh, my anxious friend whose prayers have not been answered, God invites you to the intimacy of spiritual sonship.

May 11

...through endurance and the encouragement of the Scriptures we might have hope.

ROMANS 15:4, NIV

C. S. Lewis, in *Christian Behavior*:
"If you read history, you will find that the Christians who did most for the present world were those who thought most of the world to come. Aim at heaven and you will get earth thrown in. Aim at earth and you will get neither."

August 22

No man can serve two masters:
for either he will hate the one,
and love the other; or else he will hold
to the one, and despise the other.

MATTHEW 6:24

God gives people the freedom to choose.
If you sense a longing for God, a desire to
change and be a new person, that's God
speaking to your heart. And when you
respond to Him, God will change you.
Make a choice for Christ now.

May 12

For whether we live, we live unto the Lord;
and whether we die, we die unto the Lord:
whether we live therefore, or die,
we are the Lord's.

ROMANS 14:8

The death of the righteous is no accident.
Do you think that the God whose
watchful vigil notes the sparrow's fall and
who knows the number of hairs on our
heads would turn His back on one of His
children in the hour of peril?

August 21

Freely ye have received, freely give.
MATTHEW 10:8

Life itself, every bit of health that we enjoy, every hour of liberty and free enjoyment, the ability to see, to hear, to speak, to think, and to imagine—all this comes from the hand of God. We show our gratitude by giving back to Him a part of that which He has given to us.

May 13

Clothe yourselves with the Lord Jesus Christ, and do not think about how to gratify the desires of the sinful nature.

ROMANS 13:14, NIV

Christ must be vitally real to us if we are to remain faithful to Him in the hour of crisis. And who knows how near that hour may be? Things are happening fast! The need for a turning to God has never been more urgent.

August 20

If any man serve me, let him follow me;
and where I am, there shall also
my servant be: if any man serve me,
him will my father honour.

JOHN 12:26

The invitation to discipleship is the most
thrilling ever to come to mankind. Just
imagine being a working partner with God
in the redemption of the world!

May 14

*So no one can become my disciple
unless he first sits down and
counts his blessings—and then
renounces them all for me.*

LUKE 14:33, TLB

This is the ultimate proof that one is
a disciple: if he follows the commands
of his teacher. Jesus said that he that
keeps God's commandments is the one
who truly loves God. Are you a
disciple of the Lord Jesus?

August 19

The Son of Man came eating and drinking, and they say, 'Here is a glutton and a drunkard, a friend of tax collectors and "sinners."' But wisdom is proved right by her actions.

MATTHEW 11:19, NIV

To be sure, we must deplore wickedness and wrongdoing, but our commendable intolerance of sin too often develops into a deplorable intolerance of sinners.
Jesus hates sin but loves the sinner.

May 15

Present your bodies a living sacrifice,
holy, acceptable unto God, which
is your reasonable service.

ROMANS 12:6

These bodies of ours are intended to
be temples of the Spirit of God. We are
to present them wholly to God as a
"living sacrifice." Our dress, our
posture, our actions should all be
for the honor and glory of Christ.

August 18

Come unto me...and I will give you rest.
MATTHEW 11:28

When we rest, we place our confidence in something outside of ourselves.
Jesus gives us the confidence we need to escape the frustration and chaos of the world around us. Rest in Him and do not worry about what lies ahead. Jesus Christ has already taken care of tomorrow.

May 16

O the depth of the riches both of the wisdom and knowledge of God! how unsearchable are his judgments, and his ways past finding out!

ROMANS 11:33

We do not understand the intricate pattern of the stars in their courses, but we know that He who created them does, and that just as surely as He guides them, He is charting a safe course for us.

August 17

Take my yoke upon you, and learn of me;
for I am meek and lowly in heart:
and ye shall find rest unto your souls.

MATTHEW 11:29

I must yield to Him...
surrender to Him...
give Him control of my life.
Through that surrender I will
find happiness!

May 17

We know that in everything God works for good with those who love him, who are called according to his purpose.

ROMANS 8:28, RSV

Christ is the answer to sadness and discouragement. He can put a spring in one's step and give one a thrill in his heart and a purpose in his mind. Optimism and cheerfulness are products of knowing Christ.

August 16

Let this mind be in you,
which was also in Christ Jesus.

PHILIPPIANS 2:5

The human mind cannot be a vacuum. It
will be filled either with good or evil. It will
be either carnal or Christlike. We can
control the kind of thoughts that enter
our minds. Some unknown wise man has
suggested: "Give your mind to Christ that
you may be guided by His wisdom."

May 18

For we know not what we should pray for as we ought: but the Spirit itself maketh intercession for us with groanings which cannot be uttered.

ROMANS 8:26

That "the Spirit itself maketh intercession" indicates that it is actually God pleading, praying, and mourning through us. Thus we become co-laborers with God, actual partners with Him.

August 15

*"Take my yoke upon you, and
learn from me."*
MATTHEW 11:29, RSV

What are the required courses in the
university of life? You are going to have to
face life; you are going to have to face
death; you are going to have to face
judgment. You can't really face any of
them without Christ.

May 19

*I consider that our present sufferings are
not worth comparing with the glory that
will be revealed in us.*

ROMANS 8:18, NIV

Affliction can be a means of refining and
of purification. Many a life has come forth
from the furnace of affliction more
beautiful and more useful. Affliction may
also be for our strengthening and
Christian development. We learn through
the trials we are called upon to bear.

August 14

The kingdom of heaven is like treasure hidden in a field, which a man found and covered up; then in his joy he goes and sells all that he has and buys that field.

MATTHEW 13:44, RSV

There is a sense in which the kingdom of God is already here in the living presence of Christ in the hearts of all true believers. There is also, however, the ultimate consummation of all things, which is called the kingdom of God.

May 20

The Spirit itself beareth witness with our spirit, that we are the children of God.

ROMANS 8:16

Because Christ rose from the dead, we *know* that sin and death and Satan have been decisively defeated. And because Christ rose from the dead, we *know* there is life after death, and that if we belong to Him we need not fear death or hell.

August 13

> *"Where did this man get this wisdom and these mighty works? Is not this the carpenter's son?"*
>
> MATTHEW 13:54-55, RSV

Jesus' teaching was unique. He took God out of the theoretical realm and placed Him in the practical. He spoke with authority! He spoke with finality! He spoke as though He knew...and He did! Am I listening to Him—or am I a cynic as were so many of His countrymen?

May 21

For you did not receive a spirit that makes you a slave again to fear, but you received the Spirit of sonship. And by him we cry, "Abba, Father."

ROMANS 8:15, NIV

Those who love Christ have that confidence in Him that raises them above fear. When I understand that Christ in His death gained a decisive victory over death and over sin, then I lose the fear of death.

August 12

And when he had sent the multitudes away, he went up into a mountain apart to pray: and when the evening was come, he was there alone.

MATTHEW 14:23

History has been changed time after time because of prayer. I tell you, history could be altered and changed again if people went to their knees in believing prayer.

May 22

I do not understand my own actions.
For I do not do what I want, but I do the
very thing I hate.

ROMANS 7:15, RSV

Self-analyzation can lead to depression.
We need to keep our attention
focused on Christ.

August 11

Then they...came and worshipped him,
saying, Of a truth thou art the Son of God.

MATTHEW 14:33

Jesus Christ is who He said He is:
God in human form. And that is a
crucial truth which undergirds the reality
of our salvation. Only the risen and
ascended Son of God is worthy of our
worship and our service.

May 23

*For the wages of sin is death; but the gift
of God is eternal life through
Jesus Christ our Lord.*

ROMANS 6:23

If we in the church want a cause to fight,
let's fight sin.

August 10

Then said Jesus unto his disciples,
if any man will come after me, let him
deny himself, and take up his cross,
and follow me.

MATTHEW 16:24

The effective Christians of history have
been men and women of great personal
discipline. To be a true, effective
disciple of Christ, we must seek to
discipline our lives and endeavor to walk
even as He walked.

May 24

*Know ye not, that to whom ye yield
yourselves servants to obey,
his servants ye are to whom ye obey;
whether of sin unto death, or of
obedience unto righteousness?*

ROMANS 6:16

Instead of filling your mind with
resentments, humbly give all over to God.
Your conflicts will diminish and your
inner tensions will often vanish. Then
your life will begin to count for something.

August 9

*Great peace have they who love your law,
and nothing can make them stumble.*

PSALM 119:165, NIV

God has sent His Son, Jesus Christ, to
the cross as a demonstration of His love
and mercy. He asks us to come to that
cross in a repentance of our sins and
submission of our will to Him. He
promises a peace treaty for all who
will come by faith. Do you have
Christ's peace in your life?

May 25

*Neither yield ye your members as
instruments of unrighteousness unto sin:
but yield yourselves unto God,
as those that are alive from the dead,
and your members as instruments of
righteousness unto God.*

ROMANS 6:13

Our human frame is often a rebellious
and unruly servant. Only through rigid
discipline are we able to master it into
complete subjection to Christ.

August 8

For whosoever will save his life shall lose it: and whosoever will lose his life for my sake shall find it.

MATTHEW 16:25

Jesus Christ spoke frankly to His disciples and hid nothing from them. In unmistakable language He told them that discipleship meant a life of self-denial and the bearing of a cross. He asked them to count the cost carefully.

May 26

Death no longer has mastery over him.
ROMANS 6:9, NIV

Nothing can harm us, including death,
when we have trusted Christ as
Savior because Christ has conquered
death—and so shall we.

August 7

For the Son of man shall come in the glory of his Father with his angels; and then he shall reward every man according to his works.

MATTHEW 16:27

Christians are joint heirs with Jesus Christ through redemption, which is made theirs by faith in Him based on His death at Calvary.

May 27

I am the resurrection, and the life: he that believeth in me, though he were dead, yet shall he live.

JOHN 11:25

Upon what is hope based? It is based upon the resurrection of Jesus Christ.

August 6

*Wherefore comfort one another
with these words.*

1 THESSALONIANS 4:18

The Scripture says that in the midst
of persecution, confusion, wars, and
rumors of wars, we are to comfort one
another with a knowledge that Jesus
Christ is coming back in triumph,
glory, and majesty.

May 28

Knowing this, that our old man is crucified with him, that the body of sin might be destroyed, that henceforth we should not serve sin.

ROMANS 6:6

The cross, where Christ died in our place and where we can find forgiveness, is the only place to find forgiveness and have eternal life. Because Christ lives, I live also if I am in Him and He is in me.

August 5

It is easier for a camel to go through the eye of a needle, than for a rich man to enter into the kingdom of God.

MATTHEW 19:24

The world's favorite verb is "get."
The verb of the Christian is "give."
Self-interest is basic in modern society.
But in God's kingdom self-interest is not
basic—selflessness is.

May 29

Since we have now been justified by his blood, how much more shall we be saved from God's wrath through him!

ROMANS 5:9, NIV

The saved person is in God's safety zone,
cleansed by the blood of Christ.
The one who takes his stand at the Cross
is saved forevermore. He can never come
into condemnation.

August 4

The disciples came to him privately, saying, "Tell us, when will this be, and what will be the sign of your coming and of the close of the age?"

MATTHEW 24:3, RSV

One thing almost everyone who loves Jesus Christ agrees on—Jesus Christ *is* coming back. For the true believer in Jesus Christ, the future is assured. We wait the distant trumpet announcing the coming of Jesus Christ.

May 30

Greater love hath no man than this, that a man lay down his life for his friends.

JOHN 15:13

No matter what sin we have committed, no matter how black, dirty, shameful, or terrible it may be, God loves us. We may be at the very gate of hell itself, but God loves us with an everlasting love. Because of His love there is a way of salvation, a way back to God through Jesus Christ, His Son.

August 3

Therefore you also must be ready;
for the Son of man is coming at an hour
you do not expect.

MATTHEW 24:44, RSV

The return of Jesus Christ will be the
most glorious and wonderful surprise of
all for those who know Him and have
committed their lives to Him. We should
use every opportunity we have to tell
others of our glorious Savior who wants
all of us to live with Him forever.

May 31

God commendeth his love toward us,
in that, while we were yet sinners,
Christ died for us.

ROMANS 5:8

The Bible teaches that "God is love" and
that God loves you. To realize that is of
paramount importance. Nothing else
matters so much. And loving you, God
has wonderful plans for your life.

August 2

*Verily I say unto you, Inasmuch as ye did
it not to one of the least of these,
ye did it not to me.*

MATTHEW 25:45

There must be a practical outworking of
our faith here in this present world, or it
will never endure in the world to come.
We need fewer words and more charitable
works; less palaver and more pity; less
repetition of creed and more compassion.

June 1

*The love of God is shed abroad in our
hearts by the Holy Ghost
which is given unto us.*

ROMANS 5:5

Talking about the secret of Spirit-filled
living, the great evangelist, D. L. Moody,
said, "I believe firmly that the moment our
hearts are emptied of pride and
selfishness and ambition and everything
that is contrary to God's law, the Holy
Spirit will fill every corner of our hearts."

August 1

Go ye therefore, and teach all nations...
teaching them to observe all things
whatsoever I have commanded you:
and, lo, I am with you alway,
even unto the end of the world.

MATTHEW 28:19-20

This is a glorious time to be alive.
I have found that people everywhere will
respond to the gospel of Jesus Christ if
we present it simply, with compassion.

June 2

For through him we both have access by one Spirit unto the Father.

EPHESIANS 2:18

We are not worthy to approach the holy throne of God except through Jesus Christ. The person who comes with confidence to the throne of grace has seen that his approach to God has been made possible because of Jesus Christ.

July 31

I will be with you always,
to the very end of the age.
MATTHEW 28:20, NIV

We can count on Christ's presence not only every day, but every moment of every day. Of the *fact* of His presence there can be no doubt, for His Word cannot fail. What we need is to cultivate the *sense* of His presence, every day, every hour, every moment.

June 3

By whom also we have access by faith into this grace wherein we stand, and rejoice in hope of the glory of God.

ROMANS 5:2

Charles Haddon Spurgeon shares, "The man who knows that his hope of glory will never fail him because of the great love of God, of which he has tasted, that man will hear music at midnight; the mountains and the hills will break forth before him into singing wherever he goes."

July 30

I will not leave you comfortless.

JOHN 14:18

Suffering is endurable if we do not have
to bear it alone; and the more
compassionate the Presence,
the less acute the pain.

June 4

Therefore being justified by faith,
we have peace with God through our
Lord Jesus Christ.

ROMANS 5:1

There is no conflict in the heart where
Christ abides, for His words,
"Peace I leave with you" (John 14:27),
have been proven in the test tubes of
human experience over and over again,
in the lives of those who have
trusted His grace.

July 29

And when he had sent them away, he departed into a mountain to pray.

MARK 6:46

Jesus was never too hurried to spend hours in prayer. He prayed before every difficult task confronting Him. He prayed with regularity—not a day began or closed on which He did not unfold His soul before His Father. Never stop praying no matter how dark and hopeless your case may seem.

June 5

For they exchanged the truth...
for a lie, and worshiped and served the
creature rather than the Creator,
who is blessed forever. Amen.

ROMANS 1:25, NASB

The very presence of counterfeits proves
the existence of the real. There would be
no imitations without a genuine product.
God's original design has always had
imitators and counterfeits!

July 28

For from within, out of the heart of man come evil thoughts, fornication, theft, murder, adultery, coveting, wickedness, deceit, licentiousness, envy, slander, pride, foolishness. All these evil things come from within, and they defile a man.

MARK 7:21-23, RSV

Jesus indicated that our problem is heart trouble. To have a spiritual awakening, the cross of Jesus Christ must be central in all teaching, preaching, and practice.

June 6

And herein do I exercise myself,
to have always a conscience void of
offence toward God, and toward men.

ACTS 24:16

Conscience is God's lamp within man's
breast. Its very existence within us is
a reflection of God in the soul of man.
Our consciences can be purified as we
allow God's Word, the Bible, to clean
and enlighten them.

July 27

Whosoever will save his life shall lose it;
but whosoever shall lose his life for my
sake and the gospel's, the same
shall save it.

MARK 8:35

Surrender is the secret of victorious
Christian living. There needs to be
confession of sin and a complete yielding
of every area of life, personality,
and will to Jesus Christ—plus faith that
Christ will accept that commitment.

June 7

Believe on the Lord Jesus Christ,
and thou shalt be saved.

ACTS 16:31

Many have been told to look for
spiritual thrills, but the Bible says that
"a man is justified by faith,"
and not by feeling. A man is saved by
trusting in the finished work of
Christ on the Cross and not by bodily
sensations and religious ecstasy.

July 26

*For the Son of man also came not
to be served but to serve, and to give
his life as a ransom for many.*

MARK 10:45, RSV

God can use a sensitive Christian
to be a rich blessing in the life of one
who knows pain and sorrow.

June 8

They returned...strengthening the souls
of the disciples, exhorting them to
continue in the faith, and saying that
through many tribulations we must
enter the kingdom of God.

ACTS 14:22, RSV

Christians can rejoice in tribulation
because they have eternity's values in
view. When the pressures are on, they
look beyond their present predicament to
the glories of heaven.

July 25

What things soever ye desire, when ye pray, believe that ye receive them, and ye shall have them.

MARK 11:24

With God nothing is impossible. No task is too arduous, no problem is too difficult, no burden is too heavy for His love. The future is fully revealed to Him. We must learn the difficult lesson of praying as the sinless Son of God Himself prayed, "Not my will, but thine, be done."

June 9

*The disciples were filled with joy,
and with the Holy Ghost.*

ACTS 13:52

If you know Christ and have committed
your life to Him, learn from Him and live
a consistent life for Him. Do others see
something of Christ—His love, His joy,
His peace—in your life?

July 24

But Jesus often withdrew to lonely places and prayed.

LUKE 5:16, NIV

The precious hours of fellowship with his heavenly Father meant much more to our Savior than sleep, for the Bible says, "Jesus went out into the hills to pray, and spent the night praying to God" (Luke 6:12, NIV).

June 10

And Peter came to himself, and said,
"Now I am sure that the Lord has sent
his angel and rescued me from
the hand of Herod."

ACTS 12:11, RSV

Thank God for the angelic forces
that fight off the works of darkness.
Angels never minister selfishly;
they serve so that all glory may be given
to God as believers are strengthened.

July 23

If any man will come after me, let him deny himself, and take up his cross daily, and follow me.

LUKE 9:23

We Christians should dare to be different! Jesus' disciples influenced thousands to embrace the Christian faith because they out-thought, out-lived, and out-loved their neighbors.

June 11

And whatsoever ye shall ask in my name, that will I do, that the Father may be glorified in the Son.

JOHN 14:13

Our prayer must be for God's glory. If we are to have our prayers answered, we must give God the glory.

July 22

Consider the ravens: They do not sow or reap...yet God feeds them. And how much more valuable you are than birds!

LUKE 12:24, NIV

We can be certain and worry-free about God's love, protection, and provision because He has never gone back on a single one of His promises. He never changes. Great is His faithfulness.

June 12

And when they had prayed, the place was shaken where they were assembled together; and they were all filled with the Holy Ghost, and they spake the word of God with boldness.

ACTS 4:31

To be filled with the Spirit is to be controlled by the Spirit. It is to be so yielded to Christ that our supreme desire is to do His will.

July 21

Be filled with the Spirit.

EPHESIANS 5:18

We ought to be men and women who are
living disciplined lives, men and
women who are following Christ in a
Spirit-filled life. Having had your
heart cleansed by the blood of Christ,
having submitted and yielded every area
of your life to Him, you can claim by
faith to be filled with the Spirit.

June 13

Neither is there salvation in any other: for there is none other name under heaven given among men, whereby we must be saved.

ACTS. 4:12

The one and only way you can be converted is to believe on the Lord Jesus Christ as your own personal Lord and Savior. You can come "just as you are."

July 20

For which of you, intending to build a tower, sitteth not down first, and counteth the cost...?

LUKE 14:28

Christ calls us to follow Him, regardless of the cost, and He has never promised that our path will always be smooth.

I have chosen Christ not because He takes away my pain but because He gives me strength to cope with that pain and in the long range to realize victory over it.

June 14

This Jesus God raised up,
and of that we all are witnesses.
ACTS 2:32, RSV

God, through the refining fire of
His Spirit, performs a thousand miracles
a day in the spiritual realm. His
regenerating power is ever at work in the
world, taking the ashes of burned-out
lives and changing them to dynamic
channels, dedicated to winning the
salvation of others!

July 19

There is joy before the angels of God over one sinner who repents.

LUKE 15:10, RSV

Not only does God love you, but the angels love you too. They are anxious for you to repent and turn to Christ for salvation before it is too late. They know the terrible dangers of hell that lie ahead. They want you to turn toward heaven, but they know that this is a decision that you and you alone will have to make.

June 15

*They were all filled with
the Holy Spirit.*
ACTS 2:4, RSV

The early church had no church
buildings, no Bibles, no automobiles, no
planes, no trains, no television, no radio.
Yet they turned their world "upside down"
for Christ. They instituted a spiritual
revolution simply because they were
filled with the Spirit.

July 18

No servant can serve two masters:
for either he will hate the one, and love
the other; or else he will hold to the one,
and despise the other. Ye cannot serve
God and mammon.

LUKE 16:13

Too often, *things* become our focus of
worship. It is at that point that material
goods become our masters rather than
our servants. You must choose whom you
will serve. Will it be God or money?

June 16

These are written, that ye might believe that Jesus is the Christ, the Son of God; and that believing ye might have life through his name.

JOHN 20:31

Life is a glorious *opportunity* if it is used to condition us for eternity. If we fail in this, though we succeed in everything else, our life will have been a failure. One hundred years from this day you will be more alive than you are at this moment.

July 17

And it came to pass, that the beggar died, and was carried by the angels into Abraham's bosom.

LUKE 16:22

Even as the angels escorted Lazarus when he died, so we can assume that they will escort us when by death we are summoned into the presence of Christ.

June 17

We love him, because he first loved us.
1 JOHN 4:19

God created man with the capacity to love. Love is based upon one's right to choose to love. We cannot force others to love us. We can make them serve us or obey us. But true love is founded upon one's freedom to choose to respond.

July 16

Jesus Christ...will transform our lowly body that it may be conformed to His glorious body, according to the working by which He is able even to subdue all things to Himself.

PHILIPPIANS 3:20-21, NKJV

No matter what afflictions, pain, or distortions we have in our earthly bodies, we will be given new bodies. What a glorious promise of things to come!

June 18

I pray for them...for they are thine. And all mine are thine, and thine are mine; and I am glorified in them.

JOHN 17:9-10

After you have given yourself completely to Christ in surrender to Him, remember that God has accepted what you have presented. You have come to Him; now He has received you. And He will in no wise cast you out!

July 15

*Be joyful in hope, patient in affliction,
faithful in prayer.*
ROMANS 12:12, NIV

If there are any tears shed in heaven, they
will be over the fact that we prayed so
little. Heaven is full of answers to prayer
for which no one ever bothered to ask!

June 19

I have given them thy word; and the world has hated them, because they are not of the world, even as I am not of the world.

JOHN 17:14, RSV

Jesus dined with publicans and sinners, but He did not allow the social group to conform Him to its ways. Our social contacts should not only be pleasant, but also opportunities to share our faith with those who do not yet know Christ.

July 14

And then shall they see the Son of man
coming in a cloud with power
and great glory.

LUKE 21:27

The human race is rushing madly toward
some sort of climax, and the Bible
accurately predicts what the climax is!
God's plan was inaugurated at the first
coming of Jesus Christ. It will be
completed at His second coming!

June 20

If ye were of the world, the world would love his own: but because ye are not of the world, but I have chosen you out of the world, therefore the world hateth you.

JOHN 15:19

We should refuse to support anything which does not meet with the approval of our Christian conscience. The Christian who refuses to compromise in matters of honesty, integrity and morality is bearing an effective witness for Christ.

July 13

When these things begin to come to pass, then look up, and lift up your heads; for your redemption draweth nigh.

LUKE 21:28

That is the hope that is in the heart of every believer—that our redemption is drawing nigh. Certainly we are two thousand years nearer the coming again of the Lord Jesus Christ than we were when He made those predictions.

June 21

These things I command you,
that ye love one another.

JOHN 15:17

Love is the real key to Christian unity.
In the spirit of true humility, compassion,
consideration, and unselfishness—which
reflect the mind of the Lord Jesus—we are
to approach our problems, our work, and
even our differences.

July 12

Jesus answered him, "Truly, truly, I say to you, unless one is born anew, he cannot see the kingdom of God."

JOHN 3:3, RSV

Just as surely as God implants the life cell in the tiny seed that produces the mighty oak, and as surely as He instills the heartbeat in the life of the tiny infant yet unborn, He implants His divine life in the hearts of men who earnestly seek Him through Christ.

June 22

This is my commandment, That ye love one another, as I have loved you. Greater love hath no man than this, that a man lay down his life for his friends.

JOHN 15:12-13

Tears shed for self are tears of weakness, but tears of love shed for others are a sign of strength. Until I have learned the value of compassionately sharing others' sorrow, distress, and misfortune, I cannot know real happiness.

July 11

But seek ye first the kingdom of God, and his righteousness; and all these things shall be added unto you.

MATTHEW 6:33

Order is very important in most everything we do. By putting Jesus Christ and His will for your life first, everything else will fall into place. Try putting Christ first and watch how your life is turned around.

June 23

*He that dwelleth in the secret place of
the most High shall abide under the
shadow of the Almighty.*

PSALM 91:1

If you read and reread Psalm 91,
you will discover that in Him we have
a permanent abode and residence, and
that all of the comfort, security,
and affection which the human heart
craves is found in Him.

July 10

Will you not revive us again?

PSALM 85:6, NIV

Revival is not more and not less than
the presence of Christ in the heart,
the home, the community, and the
nation. Revival must begin with
individuals. In the words of an old hymn,
"Lord, send a revival,
and let it begin with me."

June 24

*And I will pray the Father, and he
shall give you another Comforter, that he
may abide with you for ever.*

JOHN 14:16

By faith accept the fact that you are
indwelt by the Spirit of God. He is there to
give you special power to work for Christ.
He is there to give you strength in the
moment of temptation.

July 9

Christ Jesus came into the world to save sinners; of whom I am chief.

1 TIMOTHY 1:15

Many men who have been used of God were great sinners and seemed unreachable. Don't give up on any one. There is no man beyond the grace of God.

June 25

Foxes have holes and birds of the air have nests, but the Son of Man has no place to lay his head.

MATTHEW 8:20, NIV

During Christ's ministry on earth He had no home. But His home in heaven will last forever. The early disciples and other Christian pilgrims suffered in many ways, but they were all eagerly anticipating the beauty and permanence of a never-ending home that would last throughout eternity.

July 8

God is a Spirit; and they that worship him must worship him in spirit and in truth.

JOHN 4:24

"God is a Spirit—infinite, eternal and unchangeable." Those three words beautifully describe God. Men change, fashions change, conditions and circumstances change, but God never changes. Jesus Christ is the same yesterday, today and forever.

June 26

In my Father's house are many mansions:
if it were not so, I would have told you.
I go to prepare a place for you.

JOHN 14:2

Heaven is a home which is permanent.
The venerable Bishop Ryle is reputed to
have said: "Heaven is a prepared place for
a prepared people, and they that enter
shall find that they are neither
unknown nor unexpected."

July 7

*Jesus saith unto them, My meat is to do
the will of him that sent me,
and to finish his work.*

JOHN 4:34

Covet the will of God for your life more
than anything in the world. You can have
peace in your heart with little if you are in
the will of God; but you can be miserable
with much if you are out of His will.

June 27

By this shall all men know that ye are my disciples, if ye have love one to another.

JOHN 13:35

Abraham Lincoln once said, "I feel sorry for the man who can't feel the whip when it is laid on the other man's back."

July 6

Many Samaritans from that city believed
in him because of the woman's testimony,
"He told me all that I ever did."

JOHN 4:39, RSV

No matter how sinful or unworthy we may
feel today, God can use us. Throughout
history God has chosen ordinary people
and unworthy people and the least likely
people. He can use us in our community,
our town, our city, our country!

June 28

*He that loveth his life shall lose it;
and he that hateth his life in this world
shall keep it unto life eternal.*

JOHN 12:25

We are made in the image of God.
We are made to glorify God.
We are made for God; and without God
there is an empty place in our life.
That empty place can be filled by a
simple surrender to Jesus Christ.

July 5

I tell you the truth, whoever hears my word and believes him who sent me has eternal life and will not be condemned; he has crossed over from death to life.

JOHN 5:24, NIV

God will not force the new life upon us against our will. We must be ready to receive Christ as Lord and Savior with all our hearts. Then the miracle of the new birth takes place.

June 29

If the Son therefore shall make you free,
ye shall be free indeed.

JOHN 8:36

One can have political freedom and still
be a prisoner of sin, while one who is in
a political prison and knows Christ can
be more free than his jailers. Freedom in
Christ is the ultimate freedom to be
celebrated, not only on special days,
but all year around.

July 4

For as the Father has life in himself, so he has granted the Son also to have life in himself, and has given him authority to execute judgment, because he is the Son of man.

JOHN 5:26-27, RSV

Why is Christianity so different from the religions of the world? It is because Christianity is not a religion. It is a relationship with a living God, Jesus Christ.

June 30

We wrestle not against flesh and blood, but against principalities, against powers, against the rulers of the darkness of this world, against spiritual wickedness in high places.

EPHESIANS 6:12

Satan employs every device at his command to harass, tempt, thwart, and hurt the people of God. But the Christian is not left defenseless in this conflict. God provides power to give victory over Satan.

July 3

As long as I am in the world,
I am the light of the world.
JOHN 9:5

We are holding a light. We are to let it
shine! Though it may seem but a
twinkling candle in a world of blackness,
it is our business to let it shine.
Light dispels darkness, and it attracts
people in darkness to it.

July 1

I am the door: by me if any man enter in, he shall be saved.

JOHN 10:9

God puts no price tag on the Gift of gifts—salvation is free! Money can't buy it. Man's righteousness can't earn it. Social prestige can't help us acquire it. Morality can't purchase it. It is as Isaiah quoted: "Without money and without price."

July 2